EPILEPSY
COMING TO TERMS WITH CHRONIC SEIZURES

By Simon Pierce

Portions of this book originally appeared in *Epilepsy* by Terri Dougherty.

LUCENT
P R E S S

Published in 2018 by
Lucent Press, an Imprint of Greenhaven Publishing LLC
353 3rd Avenue
Suite 255
New York, NY 10010

Designer: Deanna Paternostro
Editor: Jennifer Lombardo

Library of Congress Cataloging-in-Publication Data

Names: Pierce, Simon, author.
Title: Epilepsy : coming to terms with chronic seizures / Simon Pierce.
Description: New York : Lucent Press, [2018] | Series: Diseases and disorders
  | Includes bibliographical references and index.
Identifiers: LCCN 2017051353| ISBN 9781534562585 (library bound book) | ISBN
  9781534562868 (pbk. book) | ISBN 9781534562592 (eBook)
Subjects: LCSH: Epilepsy.
Classification: LCC RC372 .P54 2018 | DDC 616.85/3–dc23
LC record available at https://lccn.loc.gov/2017051353

Printed in the United States of America

CPSIA compliance information: Batch #CW18KL: For further information contact Greenhaven Publishing LLC, New York,
New York at 1-844-317-7404.

Please visit our website, www.greenhavenpublishing.com. For a free color catalog of all our
high-quality books, call toll free 1-844-317-7404 or fax 1-844-317-7405.

CONTENTS

Illness is an unfortunate part of life, and it is one that is often misunderstood. Thanks to advances in science and technology, people have been aware for many years that diseases such as the flu, pneumonia, and chicken pox are caused by viruses and bacteria. These diseases all cause physical symptoms that people can see and understand, and many people have dealt with these diseases themselves. However, sometimes diseases that were previously unknown in most of the world turn into epidemics and spread across the globe. Without an awareness of the method by which these diseases are spread—through the air, through human waste or fluids, through sexual contact, or by some other method—people cannot take the proper precautions to prevent further contamination. Panic often accompanies epidemics as a result of this lack of knowledge.

Knowledge is power in the case of mental disorders, as well. Mental disorders are just as common as physical disorders, but due to a lack of awareness among the general public, they are often stigmatized. Scientists have studied them for years and have found that they are generally caused by hormonal imbalances in the brain, but they have not yet determined with certainty what causes those imbalances or how to fix them. Because even mild mental illness is stigmatized in Western society, many people prefer not to talk about it.

Chronic pain disorders are also not well understood—even by researchers—and do not yet have foolproof treatments. People who have a mental disorder or a disease or disorder that causes them to feel chronic pain can be the target of uninformed opinions. People who do not have these disorders sometimes struggle to understand how difficult it can be to deal with the symptoms. These disorders are often termed "invisible illnesses" because no one can see the symptoms; this leads many people to doubt that they exist or are serious problems. Additionally, people who have an undiagnosed disorder may understand that they are experiencing the world in a different way than their peers, but they have no one to turn to for answers.

Misinformation about all kinds of ailments is often spread through personal anecdotes, social media, and even news sources. This series aims to present accurate information about both physical and mental conditions so young adults will have a better understanding of them. Each volume discusses the symptoms of a particular disease or disorder, ways it is currently being treated, and the research that is being done to understand it further. Advice for people who may be suffering from a disorder is included, as well as information for their loved ones about how best to support them.

With fully cited quotes, a list of recommended books and websites for further research, and informational charts, this series provides young adults with a factual introduction to common illnesses. By learning more about these ailments, they will be better able to prevent the spread of contagious diseases, show compassion to people who are dealing with invisible illnesses, and take charge of their own health.

A MISUNDERSTOOD DISORDER

Epilepsy—also sometimes called seizure disorder— is a disorder that, as its alternate name suggests, causes seizures, which are "sudden surge[s] of electrical activity in the brain."[1] When a person has epilepsy, they have multiple seizures. Sometimes these have a clear cause, which is known as a trigger, but other times they do not. It can take several seizures for someone to identify their trigger, and there may be multiple triggers.

According to Healthline, only about 1 percent of Americans will develop epilepsy during their lifetime. However, although this percentage is low, it represents between 2.5 and 3 million people.

What Happens in the Brain?

During an epileptic seizure, the normal electrical activity in the brain is briefly disrupted. A sudden surge of electrical activity occurs that can impact a person's senses and actions, making a person spasm, stare, or lose consciousness. Sanjay Singh, the director of the Creighton Epilepsy Center in Omaha, Nebraska, described it this way: "Brain cells talk to one another by electrical discharges. When you have an abnormal electrical discharge in the brain which causes changes in behavior, that's a seizure. It's like an electrical storm in your brain."[2]

The seizures that result from this "electrical storm"

Hippocrates was one of the only people in the ancient world to look for a natural cause for epilepsy.

have been baffling people for thousands of years. The word "epilepsy" comes from the Latin word *epilepsia*, meaning "to take hold of." During a seizure, an unknown force seems to take hold of a person's body, and at one time, people blamed these seizures on demonic possession. Although the Greek physician Hippocrates theorized in 400 BC that the seizures had a natural cause, the idea persisted that they came from a curse or psychotic disorder.

Persistent Myths

Although cases of epilepsy have been recorded for centuries and are known to result from a physical cause, many people still do not understand the disorder. "It is still oftentimes surrounded by fear and mystery,"[3] said Eric Hargis, former president and chief executive officer of the Epilepsy Foundation. Some people mistakenly believe that epilepsy is contagious or that people who tell others they have it are only looking for attention. A few people even still think it indicates demonic possession. When people have these false beliefs, they may intentionally or unintentionally treat people with epilepsy in offensive, hurtful ways.

Although medical research has determined that epilepsy is caused by misfiring neurons in the brain and is not a mental illness or contagious, misperceptions about epilepsy persist. People with this seizure disorder may be labeled as "epileptics," when the preferred term is "people with epilepsy." Some people mistakenly think people with epilepsy are mentally challenged, but most people with the disorder have average intelligence. Still others think epilepsy is untreatable. Many do not realize that it is not always a lifelong illness, and that there are medications and other treatments that can control seizures—although treatment is not the same thing as a cure, and not every case of epilepsy is treatable.

The lack of knowledge about epilepsy by the general public is only one challenge faced by people with epilepsy, however. The condition continues to pose physical challenges as a person with epilepsy faces the possibility of a life disrupted by seizures that may not be controllable. Much progress has been made, and the majority of people with epilepsy can have their seizures controlled by medication, surgery, or other means. However, many people with epilepsy are still seeking freedom from seizures or the frustrating side effects of their medication. Some answers have been found, but there is still much to learn about the brain and what happens when its electrical connections misfire.

CHAPTER ONE

WHAT IS EPILEPSY?

Epilepsy is a seizure disorder that can cause people to lose consciousness, collapse and jerk, or lose awareness and just stare. It is found in all countries and affects people of all ages and ethnic groups. Worldwide, between 50 and 60 million people have epilepsy; according to the World Health Organization (WHO), this makes it one of the most common neurological disorders in the world.

Although it impacts people around the world, many people do not realize epilepsy is a common disorder. The number of people with epilepsy is more than the combined number of people who have multiple sclerosis, cerebral palsy, muscular dystrophy, and Parkinson's disease. It is estimated that between 1 and 3 percent of people develop some type of epilepsy before they are 75 years old, and the Epilepsy Therapy Project estimates that up to 5 percent of people worldwide will have a seizure at some point in their lives.

Nonetheless, epilepsy is often misunderstood. The seizures that people with epilepsy experience can be frightening and unpredictable. "Epilepsy has afflicted human beings since the dawn of our species and has been recognized since the earliest medical writings," noted one epilepsy expert. "Few medical conditions have attracted so much attention and generated so much controversy."[4]

Authors Edgar Allan Poe and Charles Dickens

had epilepsy, as did Theodore Roosevelt, the 26th president of the United States.

Part of what makes epilepsy so difficult is that its seizures may come at any time, without warning. A person does not experience the symptoms of epilepsy constantly. A person may be seizure-free for days or longer and then suddenly have another episode. The unpredictability of the condition and the unusual nature of some seizures make epilepsy challenging to live with and to treat.

Edgar Allan Poe was one of several famous historical figures who had epilepsy.

Explaining Epilepsy

It is clear that this chronic seizure disorder is rooted in the brain. A person is considered to have epilepsy after having two or more seizures that are not caused by another medical condition. When a person has a seizure, something happens in the brain that impacts the nervous system, causing it to go haywire. When things go wrong inside the brain, it can affect the way a person's body moves or their awareness of what is going on around them.

A seizure is commonly thought of as a jerking movement known as a convulsion, but many different types of seizures exist. A person may stare and be unaware of what is happening or may become confused about where they are. They may lose consciousness for a few seconds or a fraction of a second. Lip smacking, sudden jerks, a bicycling movement of the legs, picking at clothes or the air, and shaking movements can be signs that something inside the brain is causing a person to have a seizure. However, because people are unfamiliar with some of these types of seizures, they may falsely believe that they are not "real" seizures.

A Low Risk of Brain Damage

Epilepsy is the result of something going wrong inside the brain, but the seizures themselves do not generally cause long-term problems with a person's intellect or reasoning, said Roy Sucholeiki of Central DuPage Hospital in Chicago, Illinois. Although having a seizure is not good for the brain, an occasional seizure will not damage it. "There are brilliant people who have epilepsy," Sucholeiki noted. "It is not completely controlled, and they [do] not seem to have the loss of intellectual abilities over time."[1]

Epilepsy seldom causes brain damage, although a severe, prolonged seizure could cause some cognitive delay. Certain types of epilepsy are more likely to cause brain damage, noted William Davis Gaillard, the division chief of epilepsy, neurophysiology, and critical care neurology at the Children's National Health System in Washington, D.C.

If cognitive delay is noted, it may be unclear whether the epilepsy caused the problem or whether there is another, underlying problem causing both the epilepsy and other problems. "It's the chicken or the egg," Sucholeiki said. "If you have epilepsy that's that bad, there must be some underlying abnormality that's there to begin with that might cause [impairment]."[2]

1. Roy Sucholeiki, telephone interview by Terri Dougherty, May 11, 2009.
2. Sucholeiki, interview.

Epilepsy itself is not an illness; rather, it is a term that indicates that a person has recurring seizures. "Epilepsy is not a disease, it's a symptom," explained Roy Sucholeiki of Central DuPage Hospital in Chicago, Illinois. "Epilepsy by definition only means that the brain of the person has a tendency to seize, to the extent treatment is indicated. It's kind of like looking at a fever, which can be caused by many kinds of infections. Fever is not a disease, it's a symptom."[5]

Some seizures cause a person to stare blankly, as if they are daydreaming.

Getting a Diagnosis

A person with epilepsy has recurring seizures that are rooted in an underlying problem in the brain. Before diagnosing a person with epilepsy, a doctor will determine whether a person is having seizures and then look for a way to explain why the seizures are happening. A person may experience shaking of the body that is not a seizure, so the doctor will ask about how the seizures occur and what they are like. When a person is falling asleep, for example, the body may jerk slightly. This common occurrence is not a seizure.

A doctor will also ask if the seizures are a recurring problem. People with epilepsy have had two or more seizures, and often they have many of them. A person may have only one seizure but not have epilepsy. A single seizure could be caused by a stroke, infection, or brain injury, among other things. If a person does not have more than one seizure, they do not have epilepsy. However, if a person has more seizures after having a brain injury, stroke, or infection or often for an unknown reason, that person is considered to have epilepsy. The key is whether the seizure is a one-time event.

Some non-epileptic medical conditions also cause seizures, so a doctor attempting a diagnosis of epilepsy must perform medical tests to determine if a seizure may have been caused by another illness. For example, a fainting spell may cause a person to lose consciousness, and even jerk or shake, but it is caused by a drop in blood flow to the brain rather than a problem that originates in the brain. A person whose levels of salt in the bloodstream fall too low, possibly due to rigorous exercise or an illness that produces diarrhea or vomiting, may have a seizure. A glucose imbalance in the body, associated with diabetes, can produce a seizure, and a panic attack or sleep disorder may be mistaken for epilepsy. Kidney problems and liver failure can also result in seizures. These seizures disrupt the way the body is functioning but are not caused by a problem with the brain's electrical activity.

To make a diagnosis of epilepsy, a doctor will use information gathered from a number of sources. Blood tests can determine if the seizures have an environmental cause, such as exposure to lead, certain chemicals, street drugs, or alcohol. Other tests examine a person's reflexes and coordination as well as mental

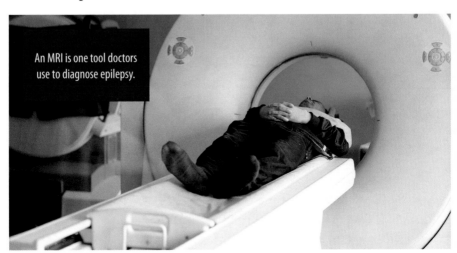

An MRI is one tool doctors use to diagnose epilepsy.

functions such as senses and memory. A person will also have an electroencephalograph (EEG) test so the doctor can look at brain waves, and brain-imaging tests such as a computerized tomography (CT) scan or magnetic resonance imaging (MRI) will allow the doctor to look at the structure of the patient's brain. Certain brain wave patterns may lead to a diagnosis of epilepsy, and the doctor will take them into account as well as the conditions surrounding a seizure and a patient's medical history when making a diagnosis of epilepsy.

Understanding How the Brain Works

It is important for doctors to look at brain waves and an image of a person's brain when making a diagnosis because they provide important clues about how the brain is functioning. Seizures begin in the brain, and looking at how a person's brain works is part of the solution to unraveling the mystery of epilepsy.

The brain is a complicated organ, with billions of nerve cells sending messages through the body to control everything a person does, including breathing, blinking, speaking, thinking, and moving. A person's conscious brain is a complex place, as the cells work together to make the body function. As the control center for the nervous system, the brain absorbs information from the senses and reacts in a fraction of a second, enabling a person to see, hear, think, and interact with others. Nerve cells provide the thoughts and reasoning that allow one to read a book or do a math problem and have the coordination needed to hit a home run or ride a bike.

The brain contains an average of 86 billion nerve cells, called neurons. At one end of each microscopic neuron are dendrites, which look like branches and reach out to gather information in the area around the cell. The dendrites are connected to the cell body.

At the other end of the nerve cell is a long, thin tail called the axon, which takes the neuron's information and passes it to other nerve cells.

A network of nerve cells in the body allows information to travel to and from the brain. To rapidly carry information from one nerve cell to another, the body uses electricity, with each nerve cell acting like a battery with electrical properties. There are gaps called synapses between the nerve cells; to send information over this gap, the nerve cells fire messages using an electrical signal. A chemical called a neurotransmitter carries this signal from one neuron to another. The message a neuron sends can quiet or excite the neuron with which it is communicating, so it gets ready to rest or fire a message itself. This method of relaying information between neurons happens in a split second, allowing the body to quickly react to all that is going on around it.

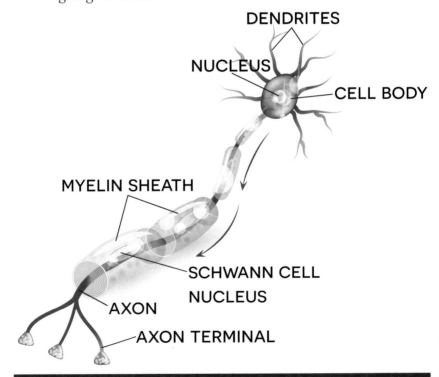

DENDRITES

NUCLEUS

CELL BODY

MYELIN SHEATH

SCHWANN CELL NUCLEUS

AXON

AXON TERMINAL

Neurons allow signals to travel throughout the brain.

To efficiently process all the information coming at it every second and distribute the necessary actions, the brain uses neural pathways. Inside the brain, the neurons are not just gathering and sending information to and from a few cells but are communicating with each other over a complex web of connections. "Each nerve cell is capable of thousands of connections with its neighbors," Sucholeiki said. "The number of connections is on the order of trillions. It's been said that there are more connections in the brain than stars in the galaxy. All these connections and networks have to have nicely balanced chemical and electrical properties."[6]

Problems occur when something disturbs this balance between the electrical and chemical properties in the brain. A tumor, stroke, something that develops at birth, or a certain drug exposure might compromise the balance between neurons. When this happens, the brain could go into a seizure.

Every second, the brain's neurons are at work, firing electrical impulses as they communicate with each other. Given the complicated nature of the brain's operations, Sucholeiki is not surprised that seizures occur, only that they do not occur more often. "By the very nature of our brain, the chance of having a seizure is not 0, it's about 9 percent," he said. "It's not necessarily surprising that the brain is capable of seizing. What's interesting is what do people, even those with epilepsy, do to keep it from seizing? Even when we sleep the brain is always turned on. It is primed for excitation."[7]

When the Brain Stops Working Correctly

As it gathers and sends information, the brain is not operating in an orderly fashion. When it is working as it should, the brain's electrical discharges are complex and disordered. Neurons are communicating with each other in a complicated way that follows no set pattern. Writer Jerry Adler described it this way:

A normal brain is governed by chaos; neurons fire unpredictably, following laws no computer, let alone neurologist, could hope to understand, even if they can recognize it on an EEG. It is what we call consciousness, perhaps the most mathematically complex phenomenon in the universe.[8]

This natural disorder comes to a halt when a person has a seizure. The normal electrical discharges in the brain become disrupted, and the brain's neurons begin firing at the same time. This may occur all over the brain at once, happen only in one area of the brain, or start in one area and spread to the rest of the brain. When the neurons start firing simultaneously, or too many neurons in one area fire at once, the body experiences a seizure. The delicate balance in the brain that has neurons sending and receiving information designed to quiet or excite other neurons becomes unhinged. "There is a fine balance in the brain between factors that begin electrical activity and factors that restrict it, and there are also systems that limit the spread of electrical activity," according to the Epilepsy Care and Research Foundation. "During a seizure, these limits break down, and abnormal electrical discharges can occur and spread to whole groups of neighboring cells at once."[9]

The impact of a seizure can vary depending on how much of the brain is impacted by the seizure and which areas of the brain are affected. The misfiring neurons may cause a person to have a staring spell that lasts only a few seconds or may make a person convulse uncontrollably for 10 minutes. Although they have different physical manifestations, any uncontrolled seizure is a serious event that poses a threat to the person with epilepsy.

In some cases, epilepsy can be fatal. In 2015, Dr. Orrin Devinsky, director of the Comprehensive Epilepsy Center at NYU Langone, said, "The public does not know that uncontrolled or ineffectively managed epilepsy leads to more than 5,000 deaths each year."[10] However, according to *Medical Daily*, that number may be much higher because people often misattribute the cause of death. For instance, a person having a seizure may be injured by falling to the floor or even by drowning in a bathtub filled with only a few inches of water, but the cause of death may be listed as the fatal injury or drowning, not a seizure. Choking on vomit is another danger. In a small number of cases, a person vomits while having a seizure; if the vomit does not drain properly from their mouth—for example, if the person is on their back and cannot roll over—they could choke.

Although it is not common, a seizure itself can cause death. A convulsive seizure that lasts longer than five minutes or multiple convulsive seizures that happen so close together that the person cannot recover between them can cause brain damage or death. When either of these things happen, it is known as convulsive status epilepticus, and the person should be immediately taken to a hospital. In the past, the length of a seizure had to be 20 minutes to be considered status epilepticus,

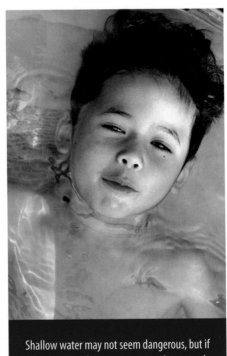

Shallow water may not seem dangerous, but if there is enough to cover someone's nose and mouth and the person is unable to control their body, the risk of drowning is high.

but doctors now know that even 5 minutes is too long. Nonconvulsive status epilepticus is also dangerous, but it does not have a specific time frame because the length and number of nonconvulsive seizures varies more widely. Additionally, the symptoms are harder for others to notice because the person does not lose consciousness or convulse; they may simply appear to be confused.

People with epilepsy are also at risk for an event called sudden unexplained death in epilepsy (SUDEP). The risk of this happening is about 1 in 1,000 each year for adults and 1 in 4,500 for children. The person is often found dead in their bed and shows no signs of having had a convulsive seizure. According to the Epilepsy Foundation, "No one is sure about the cause of death in SUDEP. Some researchers think that a seizure causes an irregular heart rhythm. More recent studies have suggested that the person may suffocate from impaired breathing, fluid in the lungs, and being face down on the bedding."[11]

How Epilepsy Affects Daily Life

Although it can be managed, epilepsy brings challenges to people's lives every day. People with epilepsy must learn to cope with the unpredictable seizures that can impact what they do. For instance, adults may not be allowed to drive a car for a number of months after having a seizure, limiting their mobility and independence. Each state has different laws regarding this, often depending on the type, number, and cause of a person's seizures. A person's career choices may be impacted by the possibility that they may suffer a seizure. In addition, there are a number of social implications and misunderstandings about epilepsy. "Part of the problem with it is not so much that it's not well known, but that it's extremely stigmatizing," Sucholeiki said. "It's somewhat taboo for

Erasing a Stigma

Epilepsy can affect anyone, and many famous as well as non-famous people have had it. However, its impact is often underestimated, and the condition is not something that is often discussed. At one time, people with epilepsy were not allowed to marry or have children. In the past, people tried to hide the disease because of its stigma, or negative perception, and the misunderstandings about the disorder.

"People have not been willing to talk about epilepsy ... I think there's a historic stigma which ... goes back to the perhaps understandable reactions people historically had to seeing somebody experience a seizure,"[1] noted Warren Lammert, cofounder and former chairman of the Epilepsy Therapy Project, which is now part of the Epilepsy Foundation.

Education about something is the only way to get rid of a stigma. When the disorder is truly understood, people with epilepsy will no longer be feared. Celebrities have traditionally had the most success in shedding light on misunderstood topics such as anxiety, depression, and chronic pain disorders. Some celebrities who have spoken out about their epilepsy include rapper Lil Wayne, actor Danny Glover, and former NFL player Alan Faneca, who was a spokesperson for the Epilepsy Foundation. These three and more have not let epilepsy stop them from having fulfilling careers.

Lil Wayne has spoken out about having epilepsy, which has made people more aware of the condition.

1. Quoted in "Living with the Uncertainty of Epilepsy," National Public Radio, April 28, 2009. www.npr.org/templates/transcript/transcript.php?storyId=103577442.

a family to talk about it; there is a lot of shame. That creates an almost unique social problem associated with the medical problem."[12]

People with epilepsy often face unnecessary hurdles because most people know so little about the condition. Although epilepsy is not contagious, sometimes a parent is unnecessarily concerned that one child will get it from another. "Most people don't think that way, but it's common enough that I need to explain it to the average patient who comes in so that [misunderstanding] is cleared up,"[13] Sucholeiki said.

People with epilepsy also must deal with ignorance about the disorder when they look for a job. The unemployment rate for employable people with epilepsy is two to three times that of the national average; for people whose epilepsy is uncontrolled, the unemployment rate may be as much as 50 percent. Eric Hargis, former president and chief executive officer of the Epilepsy Foundation, sees a lack of understanding about epilepsy contributing to this rate. "If they're not aware of what the ramifications of epilepsy actually are, they are going to be very inclined not to hire people,"[14] he said. In other words, employers who do not know much about the disorder may think someone with epilepsy will not be a good worker or will be a danger to themselves or others on the job.

The Americans with Disabilities Act (ADA) protects people with disabilities in public places, such as stores, restaurants, and other businesses; in schools; in after-school and weekend activities; and at their job. The ADA protects employees and people who are seeking jobs to a certain degree; for instance, it is illegal for a potential employer to ask a job candidate whether they have epilepsy, and candidates are not required to disclose that information before being offered a job. If someone discloses this information after they are offered the job, the employer is not allowed to revoke the job offer as long as the person is able to do all the basic functions of the job. Jobs and schools are also required to provide accommodations to someone with epilepsy, such as breaks to take medication and a private place to recover after a seizure. This law goes a long way toward protecting the rights of someone with epilepsy, but employers sometimes find ways around the law and may find another excuse for firing or not hiring someone if they find out that person has epilepsy. Additionally, sometimes a person's seizures make them unable to perform certain kinds of work; for instance, it may be hard for them to be a delivery driver if their state laws say they cannot drive for several months after having a seizure.

Additionally, many police officers do not know how to recognize seizures, which can be a problem for people with epilepsy. The police may think the person is behaving strangely due to mental illness or drug use, which can lead to people being arrested. People who have nonconvulsive seizures, which cause them to become confused and unaware of their actions, may do things such as accidentally walking out of a store with a product in their hands, which can lead to a shoplifting charge. Although a charge may be dropped if the person can get a doctor to confirm their epilepsy, the wrongful arrest causes the person distress and anxiety as well as keeping the police from arresting real criminals. Sometimes the police try to restrain someone who is having a convulsive seizure, believing the person is trying to resist arrest or attack an officer. This can lead to the person's injury or death. To combat these problems, Epilepsy Scotland started an awareness program for Scottish police officers to show them what a seizure looks like and how to handle the situation. Other countries may benefit from similar programs.

In some cultures, religious views about epilepsy stigmatize people with the disorder. Former California congressman Tony Coelho's parents, who

If police are not well trained in how to recognize seizures, they may arrest people who are not doing anything wrong.

were Portuguese immigrants, did not accept the fact that their son had epilepsy when he was diagnosed as a teen. They believed epilepsy was the result of possession by the devil. Coelho wanted to become a priest, but he was denied admission to the Jesuit seminary because of his epilepsy. He was also refused admission into the U.S. Army. He later served in Congress and became chairman of the Epilepsy Foundation board, where he worked to break down the stigma carried by epilepsy. He drew on his experiences as he sponsored the passage of the Americans with Disabilities Act. Coelho said, "What I once considered a curse forced me to face life, shaped me and strengthened me. Above all, it gave me a mission as an advocate for people with disabilities."[15]

Many epilepsy organizations are working to remove the stigma from the disorder. Part of the misunderstanding may stem from a desire for families to try to keep the condition a secret. "Epilepsy is often kept in the shadows," Hargis said. "We have parents who are stigma coaches, who tell their children, 'Don't let anyone at school know.' You don't have parents of children with asthma or diabetes tell[ing] children that."[16] Offering information about the facts of epilepsy can help that stigma disappear, he noted, and help people understand the seizure disorder rather than fear it. "There is a whole impact on quality of life you don't necessarily see with other chronic conditions," Hargis said. "The goal here is to have epilepsy recognized as a medical condition that for most people is treatable."[17]

Controlling Seizures

For people with epilepsy, controlling their seizures is the best way to minimize the impact the disorder has on their life as well as reduce the risk of SUDEP. According to the Epilepsy Foundation, control involves the following:

- *Taking your seizure medication consistently and at the right dose.*

- *Seeing your epilepsy doctor and other health care providers regularly.*

- *Ensure you are getting enough sleep each night.*

- *Avoid drinking too much alcohol or using recreational drugs.*

- *Know what triggers your seizures and adjust your lifestyle and environment as needed.*

- *If medicines do not work, consider other therapies such as epilepsy surgery, devices, or dietary therapy.*

- *Be a good manager! Take good care of yourself. Eat well and [get] regular exercise.*

- *Look at your stress level and how you can manage stress better.*

- *Track your seizures in your epilepsy diary. Note your triggers, when seizures occur, side effects or any medicine changes in the diary too! ...*

- *Know your risks for seizure emergencies and SUDEP. Talk to your doctor to understand your risk and make a plan.*[1]

1. Cyndi Wright, Patricia O. Shafer, and Joseph I. Sirven, "Preventing SUDEP," Epilepsy Foundation, last updated March 19, 2014. www.epilepsy.com/learn/early-death-and-sudep/sudep/preventing-sudep.

CHAPTER TWO

DIFFERENT TYPES OF SEIZURES

Seizures are rarely portrayed in the media, but when they are, it is generally one specific kind of seizure: tonic-clonic seizures, which involve convulsions and often a loss of consciousness. In the past, they were referred to as grand mal seizures, but today, the term tonic-clonic is preferred by experts. Because these seizures get the most attention, people may not recognize other types of seizures and may even believe nonconvulsive seizures are not real because the person looks like they are just "zoning out" for a minute.

In addition to not knowing about the different types of seizures, people are often unaware of what to do during a seizure. In some cases, they try to help when the person does not need or want help; in others, they do something potentially dangerous because they are unaware of the correct aid to offer a person who is having a seizure. For instance, one myth that has become widespread is that a person should put a spoon in the mouth of someone who is having a seizure to prevent them from swallowing their tongue. Not only is it impossible for a person to swallow their tongue, since it is attached to the jaw, putting something in a seizure patient's mouth is rude at best and dangerous at worst. The *New York Times* explained:

> *Ryan Brett, the director of education for the Epilepsy Institute in New York, said people who witness a seizure often reach for a wallet, a spoon, or a dirty object to stick in the person's mouth, much*

to the chagrin [displeasure] of epilepsy patients. He said he frequently conducted first-aid workshops in which he had to disabuse people of the myth.

"The only thing that happens when something is put in the mouth is you end up cutting someone's gums or injuring the teeth," he said. "We get complaints all the time."[18]

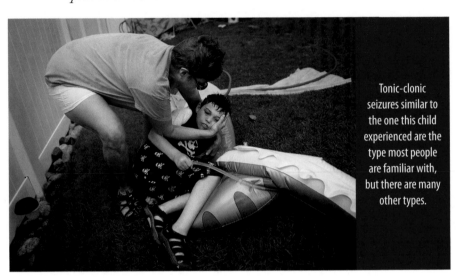

Tonic-clonic seizures similar to the one this child experienced are the type most people are familiar with, but there are many other types.

Learning more about the types of seizures can help people know when and how to give first aid to someone experiencing one.

More Than One Cause

Epilepsy most commonly begins before a person is 25 years old or after age 60. In the case of younger patients, this is because the brain is more susceptible to seizures when it is not fully developed. There are a number of things that can impact a child's brain and bring on seizures.

Sometimes an abnormality in the brain that leads to epilepsy is present at birth. The disorder also may be caused by a lack of oxygen at birth, a head injury that brings on scarring, or an illness. There may be physical causes relating to epilepsy, such as too much spinal fluid, a tumor, or a tangle of blood vessels in the brain.

Epilepsy is sometimes linked to other conditions. In children, epilepsy can be associated with autism, developmental delays, or cerebral palsy, noted Sucholeiki. A baby who is small for their age or one who has a seizure within the first month of life is also at risk for developing epilepsy. "Anything that affects the brain may put it also at risk for development of a seizure problem,"[19] Sucholeiki said.

Sometimes children have seizures when they are young but outgrow them and do not have epilepsy as adults. About 2 to 4 percent of babies and children under age 5 are prone to having seizures when they have a high fever, which are called febrile seizures. Most of these children outgrow this tendency. There are some factors that make children more likely to have multiple febrile seizures—for instance, if their parents had febrile seizures when they were young or if they have their first one before their first birthday.

Children often outgrow certain types of epilepsy as well. About 15 percent of children with epilepsy have

Some children are at risk for seizures when they have a fever.

a syndrome called benign rolandic epilepsy. Children with this type of epilepsy generally start having seizures between ages 6 and 8 and generally stop having them by they time they are 15. Children with a type of epilepsy called childhood absence epilepsy also generally outgrow their seizures. About 2 to 8 percent of children with epilepsy have this type of disorder, which generally begins between 4 and 8 years old and is often outgrown once the person reaches adulthood. Another, less common type of epilepsy that develops in young adults, called juvenile absence epilepsy, generally starts when someone is between 10 and 17 years old, but unlike childhood absence epilepsy, it is not generally outgrown. Research is ongoing to understand more about this type of epilepsy.

Benign rolandic epilepsy and childhood absence epilepsy have a genetic cause, which means children inherit their predisposition to epilepsy from their parents. Just as the way people look is a result of the combined genes they inherit from their parents, the way the cells in their brain are structured is also inherited. If a person inherits the brain-cell structure related to epilepsy, they will have a greater likelihood of developing the disorder. Juvenile absence epilepsy also has a genetic component, but less is known about genes' role in this disorder. There is not one single gene that is responsible for these forms of epilepsy; instead, they are caused by a combination of multiple genes.

If a person develops epilepsy as a young adult, a head injury is the most common cause. Although not everyone who has a head injury has recurring seizures, some people do. A car accident or a serious fall may result in a head injury that leads to epilepsy. A person in the military may begin having seizures after receiving a head injury from a bomb blast. Whether a person will get seizures after a head injury depends on what part of the head was injured, what caused the injury, and whether the person is genetically predisposed to developing epilepsy.

People in middle age who develop epilepsy may have seizures because of a head injury, stroke, or brain tumor. In people over age 65, a degenerative condition such as Alzheimer's disease or a stroke are the most common causes of epilepsy.

Although epilepsy has many causes, in a great number of cases, the reason for a person's repeated seizures is never found. Certain risk factors—such as a head injury, an infection, or having family members with epilepsy—make a person more likely to develop epilepsy; however, many people with the disorder do not have these risk factors. According to the Epilepsy Foundation, "Often we just don't know how or why epilepsy gets started."[20]

Symptoms and Their Causes

Because the brain's wiring is so complex, seizures can produce a number of symptoms. In one person, a seizure can result in convulsions, but another person may experience mental confusion. A person having a seizure may also simply stare, smack their lips, or move a hand uncontrollably.

Seizures also vary by intensity and duration, with some people experiencing mild symptoms for short amounts of time and others having longer, more violent seizures. The seizures may be so mild they are not even noticed by others or so severe that they put someone's life in danger.

One factor that has a large impact on what happens to a person during a seizure is where the seizure occurs in the brain. Different areas of the brain control different functions in the body, so the way a person acts during a seizure will depend on which areas are impacted by the misfiring neurons. However, since some things are controlled by more than one area of the brain, some seizures have similar symptoms even if they involve different areas of the brain.

Human Brain Anatomy

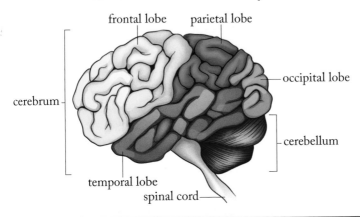

The symptoms of a seizure vary depending on which part of the brain is affected.

The temporal lobes on the sides of the head are associated with behavior, personality, and long-term memory. A person's abilities to understand language and process what someone is saying are also in this region of the brain. A person with temporal lobe epilepsy may have seizures that begin with unusual feelings or intense emotions that are not related to what is happening around them, and the seizure may include the sense that familiar people or places are strange. It also may involve random memories and hallucinations of sights, smells, or tastes. People with temporal lobe epilepsy may not understand what other people are saying, may become unresponsive, or may make unusual movements, such as smacking the lips or rubbing their hands together repetitively. Often, the seizures spread to another part of the brain and bring on convulsions.

The frontal lobe controls reasoning, judgment, decision-making, and problem-solving abilities. One part of the frontal lobe called the prefrontal cortex also controls social interaction, such as determining the appropriate behavior for a particular situation and helping people understand how others are feeling. The motor cortex area of the frontal lobe controls movement. A person may experience jerking of the thumb, for example, if the part of the brain that controls movement in that area is affected by a seizure. If the muscles that control speech are affected, a person will be unable to talk. Frontal lobe seizures may also involve the head jerking to one side, screaming, laughing, running, a bicycling movement of the legs, or an arm rising. In some cases, a person will be fully aware of what is happening around them but be unable to control their movements. A seizure that begins in the frontal lobe may not have any symptoms at all until it spreads to other areas of the brain.

A seizure may also begin in the occipital lobe in the back of the brain, which controls vision as well as unconscious decisions. A person who has a seizure that starts in the back of the brain may see images that are not really there or go temporarily blind. Their eyes may also make unusual movements, or their eyelids may flutter. After an occipital lobe seizure, between one-third and one-half of patients get a headache similar to a migraine. Seizures may also begin in the parietal lobe, which is in the center of the brain, although it is not common for seizures to begin in this area. The parietal lobe controls sensation, and a seizure that begins here may involve tingling or numbness as well as seeing or hearing things. For instance, a person may suddenly feel like one of their limbs is no longer attached to them.

Although all of these seizures involve different areas of the brain, they do have something in common. "The underlying common thread is a disturbance in the electrical and chemical properties of the brain," Sucholeiki said. "It's an abnormal and spontaneous activation of some part of the brain so you get an involuntary experience. If it's intense enough you lose consciousness of what's happening to you momentarily."[21]

A Rare Trigger

It is incredibly rare, but sometimes a person's seizures will be triggered by a song or style of music. This is called musicogenic epilepsy, and neuroscientists believe it occurs when people have an emotional reaction to music that causes a surge in the brain's electrical activity. The Epilepsy Society, an organization based in the United Kingdom (UK), reported in 2012 that it is believed to affect only 1 in 10,000,000 people. One of those people, Stacey Gayle, was 22 when she had her first seizure. Her mother took her to the hospital, but brain scans and blood tests did not reveal anything unusual. However, she continued having seizures, seemingly at random.

In 2006, about a year after her first seizure, Gayle realized that she got seizures when she heard the song "Temperature" by Sean Paul, which was very popular at the time and played often at parties and on the radio. She shared her story with *Scientific American* magazine, relating, "Every time it would go on, I would pass out and go into a seizure."[1] Over time, other songs also triggered seizures, and she had trouble going anywhere music was playing, such as a mall or airport. Eventually, she had to drop out of school because of how often people's personalized ringtones would go off in class.

Doctors prescribed her medication, but it did not work. She went through testing to determine the location of the seizures and had two operations to remove the brain cells that reacted badly to music. They found some behind her right ear—in a part of the brain involved in processing sound—as well as some in the parts of the brain that control memories and emotions.

The operations were successful, and Gayle became seizure free with no ill effects from the operations. She enrolled in school again and no longer needed to avoid music.

1. Quoted in Nikhil Swaminathan, "Musicophobia: When Your Favorite Song Gives You Seizures," *Scientific American*, June 9, 2008. www.scientificamerican.com/article/musicophobia-when-your-fa/.

Categories of Seizures

When a person has a seizure, neurons start firing at the same time. This may happen in one area of the brain, or it may start everywhere in the brain at the same time. In general, seizures are broken into three categories: generalized onset seizures, focal onset seizures, and unknown onset seizures.

When a seizure begins in one area of the brain or one group of cells, it is called a focal seizure, previously known as a partial seizure. There are two types of focal seizures: focal onset aware seizures, in which a person is awake and aware while the seizure is going on, and focal onset impaired awareness, in which a person is confused or otherwise unaware of what is going on around them. In the past, a focal aware seizure was called a simple partial seizure, while a focal impaired awareness seizure was called a complex partial seizure. According to the Epilepsy Foundation, these new terms are more accurate.

When a seizure happens over the entire brain or groups of cells on both sides of the brain at the same time, it is called a generalized onset seizure. This term has not changed. Generalized seizures include tonic-clonic, absence, atonic, and others.

Types of Epilepsy

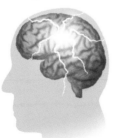 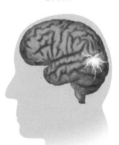

Generalized seizures affect the entire brain, while focal seizures affect only one part.

As the name implies, a seizure is classified as unknown onset when it is unclear which part of the brain the seizure started in. It can also be called unknown if no one else was there to see it and the person who had the seizure does not know exactly what happened—for instance, if it happened to someone who lives alone. It may be re-diagnosed later as either focal or generalized if more information is learned about the symptoms of that particular seizure.

The Epilepsy Foundation describes the symptoms present in different types of seizures:

For generalized onset seizures:

- *Motor symptoms may include sustained rhythmical jerking movements (clonic), muscles becoming weak or limp (atonic), muscles becoming tense or rigid (tonic), brief muscle twitching (myoclonus), or epileptic spasms (body flexes and extends repeatedly).*

- *Non-motor symptoms are usually called absence seizures. These can be typical or atypical absence seizures (staring spells). Absence seizures can also have brief twitches (myoclonus) that can affect a specific part of the body or just the eyelids.*

For focal onset seizures:

- *Motor symptoms may also include jerking (clonic), muscles becoming limp or weak (atonic), tense or rigid muscles (tonic), brief muscle twitching (myoclonus), or epileptic spasms. There may also be automatisms or repeated automatic movements, like clapping or rubbing of hands, lipsmacking or chewing, or running.*

- *Non-motor symptoms: Examples of symptoms that don't affect movement could be changes in sensation, emotions, thinking or cognition, autonomic functions (such as gastrointestinal sensations, waves of heat or cold, goosebumps, heart racing, etc.), or lack of movement (called behavior arrest).*

For unknown onset seizures:

- *Motor seizures are described as either tonic-clonic or epileptic spasms.*

- *Non-motor seizures usually include a behavior arrest. This means that movement stops— the person may just stare and not make any other movements.*[22]

Generalized Onset Seizures

When a person mentions the word epilepsy or seizure, a vision of a person having a tonic-clonic seizure generally comes to mind. This type of generalized seizure, formerly called a grand mal seizure, impacts the entire brain. It may begin with a grunt or a scream, which happens because the respiratory muscles contract involuntarily and force air past the person's vocal cords. A person loses consciousness, and the body becomes stiff because it is gripped by a muscular contraction. A person may turn pale or blue, as breathing is temporarily stopped. After a person goes through the tonic, or stiff, phase, which typically lasts for less than a minute, the clonic phase of uncontrolled jerking begins as the muscles alternately contract and relax. This may also cause them to lose control of their bladder or bowels. The seizure generally lasts a few minutes; more than five minutes is considered a medical emergency. During a tonic-clonic seizure, a person loses consciousness, and it returns slowly after the seizure ends. They may feel sleepy, disoriented, irritable, or depressed for awhile.

A person may also experience only the tonic phase. During a tonic seizure, which typically lasts no more than 20 seconds, the body's muscles tighten, causing the person to stiffen. This generally occurs only when a person is sleeping, but if it occurs when they are standing, the person often falls down. If it happens when they are awake, they may not lose consciousness or awareness. Rarely, a person will experience a clonic seizure, which involves only the jerking movements of the arms and legs; this is most common in babies.

A clonic seizure may be hard to distinguish from a myoclonic seizure—a generalized seizure that involves one or more brief jerks that last about a second. The jerking is more irregular during a myoclonic seizure than a clonic one. A person's muscles typically contract rapidly on both sides of the body. A person's arm may fly up or their foot may jerk. "Even people without epilepsy can experience myoclonus in hiccups or in a sudden jerk that may wake you up as you're just falling asleep," noted the Epilepsy Foundation. "These things are normal."[23] However, these bodily reactions are not classified as a myoclonic seizure. Rather, myoclonus describes the jerking or twitching motion of a muscle, the way someone's diaphragm muscle jerks when they have hiccups. A person with myoclonic seizures experiences abnormal movements on both sides of the body.

Whereas a person's muscles rapidly contract and relax during a myoclonic seizure, they become extremely weak during a type of generalized seizure called an atonic seizure. When a person's muscles suddenly lose strength, their body may sag. A person who is sitting down may drop what they are holding, and their head or eyelids may sag. A person who is standing will often fall to the floor and may be injured; people who are prone to atonic seizures may wear helmets to avoid getting concussions. A person generally stays conscious during these seizures, which may also be called drop attacks or drop seizures.

Some people wear seizure helmets similar to this one because repeated blows to an unprotected head can cause injury or cognitive problems.

Non-Motor Seizures

Another type of generalized seizure impacts a person's consciousness more than their muscles. Absence seizures, a well-known and common type of generalized seizure, involve sudden, momentary memory loss. A person becomes unaware of their surroundings for between 1 and 10 seconds.

The symptoms of an absence seizure, formerly known as a petit mal seizure, may be very mild or brief. With a typical absence seizure—the most common—a person suddenly stops anything they were doing and appears to be "zoning out." They may stare upward slightly for just a second, and their eyelids may flutter. They stare for a few seconds, not hearing anything going on around them, and then return to normal without realizing there had been a seizure. Atypical absence seizures are less common; they are called atypical because they often last longer and have slightly different symptoms than typical absence seizures. In this type of seizure, the person still stops their activity and stares into space, but the seizure also may involve chewing movements, lip smacking, and hand motions. While a typical absence seizure generally lasts between 1 and 10 seconds, an atypical one may last more than 20 seconds.

Epilepsy Syndromes

According to the Epilepsy Foundation, "When a disorder is defined by a characteristic group of features that usually occur together, it is called a syndrome."[1] Because epilepsy is a symptom and not its own disorder, there are many different syndromes that have epilepsy as a symptom. Syndromes have a number of characteristics in common, such as the type of seizure a person has, the behavior during the seizure, similar EEG patterns, and genetic factors. People with the same syndrome may be roughly the same age when seizures begin, have seizures that begin in the same part of the brain, and respond in similar ways to medications. If a patient's epilepsy can be classified under a certain syndrome, this can help the doctor determine which medications and treatments will work best for the patient. It can also help the doctor predict whether the patient's epilepsy will go away or lessen in severity over time.

The Epilepsy Foundation discusses 31 of these syndromes on its website. Some of them involve only one kind of seizure, while others involve multiple kinds. For instance, someone with Lennox-Gastaut syndrome often has myoclonic seizures of the neck, shoulders, upper arms, and face, as well as tonic and atonic seizures. Many epilepsy syndromes are rare.

1. Gregory L. Holmes, "Types of Epilepsy Syndromes," Epilepsy Foundation, last updated September 3, 2013. www.epilepsy.com/learn/types-epilepsy-syndromes.

About 65 percent of the time, absence seizures are outgrown by age 18. However, they can have a significant impact on a child if they remain undiagnosed before that time. Absence seizures can lead to misunderstandings if a teacher is unaware of a child's condition. A child who does not respond when a teacher calls their name may be punished for not paying attention or may be accused of disobedience. They may also miss portions of what is being taught and may be scolded for not listening if they do not understand the lesson. These seizures can happen hundreds of times a day, and if a child is not accurately diagnosed, they may be unfairly labeled as uncooperative or inattentive. "It is important to recognize that the child is not daydreaming, and is not failing to pay attention," noted Donald Weaver, the author of *Epilepsy and Seizures: Everything You Need to Know.* "He or she is genuinely unaware."[24]

Some seizures involve involuntary hand motions.

Focal Onset Seizures

Although a person having an absence seizure is unaware of what is going on around them, that is not the case with all types of seizures. A person having a focal aware seizure remains conscious and aware during the entire episode.

A focal aware seizure begins in only one area of the brain. Depending on which part of the brain is affected, the seizure may involve uncontrollable twitching, hallucinations such as a ringing sound that is not there, or abnormal sensations such as a floating or spinning feeling. A person may sweat or be nauseous, look red in the face, or feel afraid. A person may also have trouble understanding what others are saying or have trouble reading. The seizure generally lasts less than two minutes. "With a [focal] seizure, the electrical storm just involves a small part of the brain," noted Singh. "These are much more common than generalized seizures."[25]

The other type of focal seizure is a focal impaired awareness seizure, which was formerly called a complex partial seizure. A person having this type of seizure generally becomes unresponsive or unconscious. This type of seizure most often affects either the temporal or frontal lobe. During a focal impaired awareness seizure, a person's eyes may be open. However, they do not sense what is going on around them and may appear to be daydreaming. A person may make chewing motions or smack the lips, pick at clothing, make a bicycling motion with the legs, or behave oddly in other ways. These movements are called automatisms because a person does them automatically, without knowing what they are doing. Sometimes they are not fully unaware, but any effect on awareness classifies the seizure as focal impaired awareness. Other times, it is only their ability to respond that is affected; they may be aware of what is happening but unable to move or speak. "Less often, people may repeat words or phrases, laugh, scream, or cry. Some people do things during these seizures that can be dangerous or embarrassing, such as walking into traffic or taking their clothes off,"[26] according to the Epilepsy Foundation. These seizures often last one to two minutes. A person generally cannot remember the seizure afterward and may be very tired.

A focal seizure may not remain limited to one area; it may spread to another area of the brain or travel throughout the brain. Sometimes it begins with a focal aware seizure and quickly affects areas of the brain that control awareness. These are still called focal seizures because they are only affecting certain parts of the brain. When a focal seizure travels throughout the whole brain, it is called a focal to bilateral tonic-clonic seizure. Previously this type of seizure was called a

Some people feel sleepy and have trouble concentrating immediately after a seizure.

secondarily generalized seizure, and it is different than a generalized tonic-clonic seizure because it spreads to both sides of the brain rather than starting there. However, the symptoms are similar.

Stages and Triggers

Seizures have a beginning, middle, and end, although in some people, these stages are not entirely clear. Although the symptoms of a seizure are different for everyone, each person with epilepsy tends to experience seizures nearly the same way every time. A person may sense that a seizure is approaching before it happens. If this warning comes days or hours in advance, this is called the prodrome. These symptoms are not considered part of the seizure. Someone who experiences the prodrome may be able to take medication to lessen the effects or avoid certain activities that a seizure could make more harmful, such as swimming or using a ladder.

The beginning sign of a seizure is called an aura. The aura may be a feeling of dizziness or nausea, or it may be a sense of déjà vu, a feeling of lightheadedness, or even a surge of happiness. Not everyone experiences an aura; some seizures begin with no real warning. The seizure then progresses to the middle, or ictal, phase. The Epilepsy Foundation defines this as "the period of time from the first symptoms (including an aura) to the end of the seizure activity. This correlates with the electrical seizure activity in the brain."[27] The symptoms of the ictal phase vary from person to person and depend on the area of the brain that is affected by the seizure. They include confusion; loss of consciousness; hearing, seeing, or smelling things that are not there; feelings of panic; pleasant feelings; loss of awareness; tremors or convulsions; automatisms; and many more. Sometimes the symptoms last longer than the actual seizure. When this happens, the lingering symptoms are generally considered aftereffects.

After the ictal phase of the seizure, the brain begins to recover. This third stage, which is called the postictal phase, may take a few seconds, minutes, or hours. The length of the postictal phase depends on which part of the brain was affected and what type of seizure the person had. Symptoms of the postictal phase include sleepiness, memory loss, depression, embarrassment, difficulty performing normal tasks, nausea, weakness, headache, and more.

Although often it is not known exactly what provokes a seizure, sometimes a person realizes that a specific sound, sight, or condition will bring one on or make seizures occur more frequently. These conditions or sensations are called triggers.

People with reflex epilepsy have seizures after being exposed to something that stimulates a seizure. The most common type is called photosensitive epilepsy, which is triggered by flashing lights. Other types of epilepsy can be triggered by things such as reading, hearing certain noises, or smelling specific things. The Epilepsy Foundation reports that 85 percent of people with reflex epilepsy experience generalized tonic-clonic seizures in response to their trigger.

People with epilepsy may also have seizures

triggered by their physical condition. Lack of sleep or illness may trigger a seizure. Stress can also be a seizure trigger. For some people, simply falling asleep or waking up can bring on a seizure.

People with photosensitive epilepsy may not be able to attend concerts, watch certain movies or TV shows, or be in other situations that involve flashing lights.

In some cases, a nutritional deficiency—such as a lack of vitamins or minerals—may cause a seizure to occur. A person who misses a dose of medication or who takes an over-the-counter medication that decreases the effectiveness of epilepsy medication may trigger a seizure. Using drugs or heavy use of alcohol can also be a seizure trigger.

"In the vast majority of people with epilepsy, there are generally no specific triggers," Sucholeiki said. "People often report that stress will be more likely to bring one on, or perhaps sleep deprivation. In some rare cases music might provoke it, but that's more of a curiosity and very rare."[28]

A Personalized Approach

Part of what makes epilepsy such a perplexing condition is the way it impacts people with a variety of symptoms and intensities. Even among people with the same seizure syndrome or seizures that affect the same area of the brain, a wide spectrum of seizure frequency and severity exists. Additionally, the same treatment that works for one person may not work for another. This can be frustrating for patients as they try multiple therapies in an effort to find what works best.

Epilepsy can be a very individualized condition, as two people with the seizure disorder will likely experience it in very different ways. From the convulsions of a tonic-clonic seizure to the stares of an absence seizure, epilepsy can have varied physical impacts on people. The condition takes an emotional toll as well, and people with epilepsy as well as their loved ones develop their own way of coping with their seizures and the challenges epilepsy brings to their lives.

CHAPTER THREE

THE TRUTH ABOUT EPILEPSY

When people are first diagnosed with epilepsy, it may come as an unpleasant surprise. They may feel afraid at first or wonder how their lives will change. They may not yet know what their triggers are or whether they even have any. Having the support of friends and family can make this transition period less difficult. Eventually, with the help of doctors and loved ones, most people will be able to control their epilepsy.

Because of the persistence of myths and misinformation about epilepsy, many people are unsure how to react when they meet someone who has it or when a loved one is diagnosed with it. Educating themselves about the realities of the disorder can help friends and family offer real support to their loved one with epilepsy.

Getting a Diagnosis

Getting a correct diagnosis is the first step toward properly treating epilepsy. In the case of certain kinds of seizures, such as absence seizures, this can be a difficult process because they are less noticeable than seizures with motor symptoms. Additionally, epilepsy may not be the only health issue someone has, which can make it more difficult to notice.

B.J. Hamrick's family began to notice that she would have bouts of inattentiveness when she was

10, but they attributed it to illnesses that followed a rough round of strep throat. For a time, she just could not seem to get completely healthy. "I just couldn't get rid of [the strep throat]," she said. "I kept staying chronically ill after that."[29]

While they were focusing on that aspect of her health, her family did not realize that she was also showing signs of epilepsy. She would seem to "space out" as her absence seizures went untreated and her family and doctors tried to figure out what was going on. "We thought I actually had a heart problem, because my heart rate would go really high when I was having a seizure," Hamrick said. "Then we went to our family practice doctor and he took one look at one of my episodes and said, 'She's having a seizure.'"[30]

Hamrick was diagnosed with epilepsy at age 14 and began taking medication to control the seizures. She had to switch to a new medication when she built up resistance to the drug and the seizures returned. "The migraines that went hand in hand with that made it hard to function," she recalled. "It usually happened several times a week, and would be very difficult to get rid of."[31]

Her friends were supportive at first, but as time went on, Hamrick's health issues began to impact her social life. Her friends did not understand what was happening to her. "They weren't cruel or mean, but they moved on with their lives," she said.

Here I was struggling to get out of bed in the morning. You're not going to want to hang out with someone who can't even get out of bed. People would assume that if I wasn't feeling well I didn't want to spend time with them. And that wasn't true. I might have some limitations on my energy level, but I still wanted to hang out and do things.[32]

Fortunately, her older brother and sister were supportive of her as she dealt with her health issues. "I know it was hard on them sometimes because I had a lot of extra attention, but they handled it really well," she said. "My sister was really good about standing up for me and explaining things about what was happening to me."[33]

Support from family and friends can make dealing with epilepsy less difficult.

As time went on, she became close to some girls who understood her condition. "I found a core group of friends who didn't mind my limitations and wanted to hang out with me for my personality," she said. "Most were people I had grown up with and they had watched my journey."[34]

Hamrick finished high school, although it took her a little longer than others because of her health issues. She enrolled in college, found a job as a receptionist, and was pleasantly surprised when she noticed that the migraine and seizure episodes were lessening. Eventually, the seizures stopped completely. She had outgrown her epilepsy.

"I was 21 when I had my last recognizable seizure. I only get a migraine maybe once or twice a year,"

Hamrick said when she was 25. "The neurologist declared me seizure-free at 22."[35]

As Hamrick's story shows, many people do not understand the limitations that come along with a chronic problem such as epilepsy. People who want to be a good friend to someone with epilepsy should remember that the seizures may impact what a person is able to do on a daily basis. Being there for the person even when they are not feeling well is an important part of being supportive.

More Than a Pet

Most people are aware that dogs can assist the blind, but few people know they can also be trained to help people with a variety of other illnesses and disorders, including panic attacks, deafness, and epilepsy. Seizure dogs are specially trained to respond to seizures or predict when one is about to happen so the person can take precautions. The Epilepsy Foundation described some of the things seizure dogs do:

- Some dogs have been trained to bark or otherwise alert families when a child has a seizure while playing outside or in another room.

- Some dogs learn to lie next to someone having a seizure to prevent injury.

- Some dogs learn to put their body between the seizing individual and the floor to break the fall at the start of a seizure.

- Some dogs are trained to activate some kind of pre-programmed device, such as a pedal that rings an alarm.[1]

Because training dogs this way is relatively new, more research is needed to see whether certain breeds perform better as well as to identify the best way to train them. The Epilepsy Foundation warns people to thoroughly research training programs to make sure they are legitimate, especially if the training is very expensive.

Some training programs have certain requirements for people who want a seizure dog, such as requiring the person to be older than 14, have a minimum number of seizures per month, and have a stable home environment. This prevents people who do not really need the dogs or who are not able to properly care for them from adopting them.

1. "Seizure Dogs," Epilepsy Foundation, August 23, 2017. www.epilepsy.com/learn/seizure-first-aid-and-safety/staying-safe/seizure-dogs.

How to Help

It can be frightening to see a person having a seizure, and it is natural to want to help them. Although nothing can be done to stop a seizure, onlookers can do their best to make sure the person having the seizure is not injured.

While the person is having a seizure, make sure there is nothing within the person's reach that might be harmful if they were to hit it. Make the person as comfortable as possible. If the seizure occurs in a public place, keep onlookers away. Call 911 if the seizure lasts for more than 5 minutes, but do not call before that; medical care is not necessary after every seizure.

Do not try to restrain the person who is having the seizure or put anything in their mouth, as both of these actions can cause physical injuries. They should not have water, pills, or food until fully alert. Additionally, do not try to make the person "snap out of" their seizure; seizures will stop on their own, and no outside force can stop one after it has started. After the seizure, there is a small chance that the person will vomit. Place an unresponsive person on their left side, with the head turned so any vomit will come out of the mouth and reduce the person's chance of choking.

If someone is unresponsive after a seizure, roll them over onto their side in case they vomit.

The person may be confused after the seizure. It may take 5 to 20 minutes for them to recover. Stay with the person and offer support. Speak to them reassuringly and answer any questions they may have about what happened during the seizure. Do not make them feel embarrassed for having the seizure.

When speaking to a person with epilepsy, it is important to treat them like any other person. Most people with epilepsy do not need or want special treatment. Some people believe epilepsy is a mental disorder or that it affects the person's intelligence, which may make them talk down to the person. This is insulting and unnecessary. Although some forms of epilepsy are associated with cognitive disorders, the epilepsy is not the cause of the disorders, and most people who have epilepsy have normal brain function when they are not having seizures.

Some people with epilepsy are open to discussing their condition. A person who is interested in learning more from them should listen to what they say; they should not argue or try to suggest that the person is not controlling their epilepsy properly. A person's treatment choices are between them and their doctor, and most people do not welcome unasked for advice, especially from people who do not have the disorder themselves.

Learning more about epilepsy, either from someone who has it or by reading about it from reputable sources, can help people interact appropriately with a person who has epilepsy. For example, since many people are only aware of tonic-clonic seizures, they may not believe absence seizures are "real" seizures and may accuse someone of lying about having epilepsy. Others may still hold onto the outdated belief that someone who has seizures is possessed by a demon or being punished by God. Learning about the different kinds of seizures can prevent these kinds of rude, false accusations.

What Not to Say

Tiffany Kairos, who has epilepsy, put together the following list of what not to say or do when someone tells you they have epilepsy:

1. Don't raise an eyebrow and ask, "Is it contagious?"

2. Don't all of a sudden stop answering calls and texts.

3. Don't start whispering or lowering your voice to ask any questions you may have about epilepsy.

4. Don't say "That's sad!" and nothing else. This does not help.

5. Don't dismiss epilepsy as "No big deal."

6. Don't ask if the condition came from something the person did.

7. Don't say, "I know how you feel." ...

8. Don't say "Just be grateful you don't have (Insert another medical condition)." ...

9. Don't say nothing. When a friend reaches out, it makes the person with epilepsy feel wanted and needed. A lot of people are afraid and don't know what to say, but simply not saying anything can make a person feel isolated and alone.

10. Don't treat the person any differently ...

11. Don't do more for the person than they're comfortable with. Being treated like a child can be degrading. Independence is still important.[1]

Instead of these, Kairos recommended letting the person know they are still loved, asking if they need help or want to talk (but understanding if they decline the offer), offering to do specific things such as make them a meal or drive them to the doctor, and offering fun distractions when appropriate.

1. Tiffany Kairos, "18 Things to Do (and Not Do) When Someone Tells you They Have Epilepsy," The Mighty, November 20, 2015. themighty.com/2015/11/18-things-to-do-and-not-do-when-someone-tells-you-they-have-epilepsy/.

Learning to Cope

Heather Good has spent much of her life searching for a way to make her seizures go away. She has tried to control them with medication and surgery, and although she has experienced some periods of relief, the seizures have always returned.

Good was only two years old when her mother noticed that her body would get stiff just as she was falling asleep. She was hospitalized as doctors looked for a cause; while there, she had a seizure. Doctors diagnosed her with epilepsy. "I don't know how often I had them, but they always happened when I was going to sleep," Good said. "During the day I never have them … I've been on medication since I was two," she added. "A lot of the medications haven't fully worked; they're not fully controlling my seizures."[36]

Good's seizures occur while she is sleeping. Her body tenses and sometimes shakes for about a minute. Good stays sleeping during her seizure, but in the morning, she is tired and groggy.

Because medication was not taking her seizures away, Good and her family began to look at other treatment options. When Good was 13, they decided to try surgery that would remove the part of her brain that was causing the seizures. Before she had that surgery, however, doctors first needed to pinpoint the part of her brain causing her seizures. Good had an internal electroencephalograph (EEG) test, which involved a surgery to have electrodes placed on the surface of her brain. The electrodes detected her brain waves and showed where the seizure activity was occurring. Once they knew which area of her brain was having the seizures, doctors then did more tests to see if that area controlled any vital functions. "[During the tests] they give you a book to read, turn off something in your brain, and all of [a] sudden I couldn't read any more," Good said. "Or I was talking and I couldn't talk anymore."[37]

The tests showed that she had some speech and motor skills in the area where her seizures began. Surgeons could not remove the entire area, but they could safely take out some of it. The prospect of having brain surgery and a portion of her brain removed did not make Good nervous. Rather, she was excited about the possibility of having something take away her seizures. For a time, the surgery worked. "I noticed a difference for about six months after that," Good said. "Since then I haven't noticed as much of a difference."[38]

Twice a day, Good began taking three medications for her seizures. Rather than becoming less frequent, though, they started occurring more often. She often had seizures just as she was falling asleep or waking up. Good sometimes worried that her seizures would never go away or that she would have one in a public place, but she was determined not to let them define her. "I can't let my life be totally consumed by seizures and my epilepsy and how to stop it," she said. "Sometimes I tell people that epilepsy is not me, it's only one part of me. I can't let it rule my life."[39]

Support groups can help people with epilepsy connect with others who understand what they are going through.

Good found it easier to cope with her epilepsy as she got older. A teen group, sponsored by the Epilepsy Foundation, helped her realize that she was not the only person whose life was impacted by seizures:

For a long time before I joined the teen group I was ashamed of it. I was afraid of what people would think. I didn't tell people about it unless they were really close friends. But when I joined the teen group I realized that there is so much stigma surrounding epilepsy because people never talk about it, and I'm hurting the cause when I don't talk about it.[40]

Although she was no longer ashamed to have epilepsy, Good still found aspects of her condition frustrating. She began attending college for pediatric nursing, but she wished she did not have to watch her sleep schedule quite as closely as was necessary. "It's kind of frustrating in that way because I have to stop and take care of myself," she said. "It's especially hard in college, when you want to stay up and get work done."[41]

Good continued to look for something that would completely control her seizures. She tried the Atkins diet, which limits carbohydrates but allows the person to eat as much protein and fat as they want. She hoped the Atkins diet would work on the same principles as the high-fat, low-carbohydrate ketogenic diet that has worked in children with epilepsy. She also considered being part of a medical trial for a device implanted in the brain that detects seizures before they begin and uses a shock to stop them. She believes it is important for people with epilepsy to continue searching for answers. "If you sit around and pout about it, it's not going to do anything, that's my outlook," she said. "If you try to find answers and try new clinical trials and meet people with epilepsy and network, it's going to be way better for you than if you just sit around. Some people just settle, and in my mind that's not OK."[42]

Good's outlook shows that epilepsy does not have to stop someone from enjoying life. Although it can be difficult sometimes, considering the difficulties people with epilepsy face, keeping a generally positive attitude can help someone maintain as normal a life as possible.

CHAPTER FOUR

ANALYSIS AND TREATMENT

Although there is no cure for epilepsy, there are many treatments that can help control seizures. Because epilepsy varies from person to person, someone may have to try several different treatments to find the one that works best for them. Brain scans and other tests are generally done to help doctors determine which parts of the brain are affected by the person's seizures. This knowledge is necessary to help them develop a treatment plan. Medication, surgery, and implanted devices are some of the options currently available to people with epilepsy, and new research is ongoing all the time.

Electroencephalography

When deciding how to treat a person with epilepsy, doctors attempt to find what causes the seizures to occur. Information about the way the seizure impacts a person's body and which parts of the brain are involved in the seizure all help a doctor find the appropriate treatment.

The first test a person typically undergoes when epilepsy is suspected is an electroencephalograph (EEG). The EEG is a machine that has been around since the 1920s and is used to monitor a person's brain waves. The brain waves can offer important information and clues about a person's seizures. Although the brain's electrical activity is not visible, an EEG machine uses sensors to detect the brain's electrical impulses and translates this electrical activity into a set of squiggly lines. These lines are displayed on a computer monitor. The EEG readout allows a doctor to take a look at the electrical activity going on in a person's brain.

Having an EEG test is a safe and painless procedure. To gather information about the electrical activity inside a person's brain, the EEG device uses electrodes placed on a person's scalp. A number of electrodes, which are small metal disks, are attached to the scalp and have wires that are connected to an electrical box that records the brain's electrical activity. The wires do not conduct an electrical current to the scalp; instead, they simply record the electrical activity going on in the brain. The electrical box is connected to an EEG machine, which translates the electrical activity in the brain into a set of visible lines, called traces.

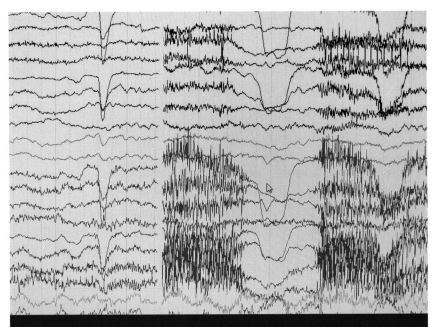

An EEG readout can show whether brain activity is normal or abnormal.
Abnormal brain activity may indicate a seizure.

The lines on the EEG readout provide information about different areas of the brain. A doctor can interpret the lines to determine if these areas are producing a normal EEG readout or if there are abnormalities that may be caused by seizures. "If it is abnormal, you can tell what kind of epilepsy someone might be having," Singh said. "It can also tell you where in the brain the seizure might be."[43]

Although certain brain wave patterns indicate that a person is likely to have epilepsy, about half of the time, the EEG readout indicates a normal brain wave pattern. This does not mean that the person does not have epilepsy, however. Abnormal brain waves may only occur during a seizure, and if a person is tested when a seizure is not occurring, the brain waves may look normal. To solve this problem, doctors may try to induce a seizure in the patient; they need to replicate the problem so they can attempt to solve it. They may try things such as flashing lights at a patient or asking if they can identify another trigger.

If the EEG test looks normal and a seizure cannot be induced, the doctor will use other information to make an epilepsy diagnosis. A description of the seizure, provided by the person being tested or a friend or relative who saw the seizure, is important. A person's medical history, which would include information about head injuries or illnesses that may have caused an infection in the brain, is another tool used by doctors when diagnosing epilepsy.

Magnetoencephalography

Magnetoencephalography (MEG) is also used to look at brain activity and help pinpoint the location of a seizure. It is similar to an EEG; the main difference is that "the skull and the tissue surrounding the brain affect the magnetic fields measured by MEG much less than they affect the electrical impulses measured by EEG. This makes the MEG more accurate than an EEG in some ways."[44] The electrical currents in the brain produce tiny magnetic fields, and the MEG provides a picture of what these magnetic fields look like.

"Instead of the 20-channel EEG, this is 306 channels," Singh said. "It is so accurate that if you move your index finger, it will tell you exactly from where in the brain the movement came from."[45]

The information gathered from the MEG is combined with information about the brain's structure, which is provided by magnetic resonance imaging (MRI). The MRI uses a powerful magnet to produce an image. This test is done to see if the person's epilepsy is the result of brain damage.

How to Read an EEG

In addition to seizures, abnormal EEG readouts can be caused by conditions related to head trauma, strokes, or brain tumors. Some brain wave patterns are typical of epilepsy, however. If a doctor sees spikes and sharp waves on an EEG readout, they may indicate that the part of the brain producing this activity is the source of a person's seizures.

Figuring out exactly what the bumpy lines on an EEG readout mean is a skill acquired by trained neurologists, who know which types of lines signal abnormalities and which changes in the readout are caused by things such as patients opening their eyes or closing their mouths. A doctor also takes other information about a patient into account when looking at the EEG readout. "Interpreting EEGs also involves some subjectivity and judgment," noted the Epilepsy Foundation.

What one interpreter reads as sharp waves may be read as spikes by another. Both may be considered correct, depending on the criteria they apply. Experienced neurologists also learn to interpret the EEG in light of the patient's medical history, physical examination, and other laboratory studies.[1]

1. Steven C. Schachter and Joseph I. Sirven, "Where It's Performed," Epilepsy Foundation, August 22, 2013. www.epilepsy.com/learn/diagnosis/eeg/where-its-performed.

Other Tests

As part of the epilepsy testing, a doctor may order blood tests. One of these is called a complete blood count (CBC). This helps doctors check for allergies or infections, which is important information when prescribing anti-seizure medication. Another type of blood test is called a chemistry panel or complete metabolic panel. A chemistry panel measures the body's levels of sodium, potassium, and blood sugar. A complete metabolic panel measures not only those, but also

Sometimes a blood test can tell doctors what is causing a person's seizures.

how well a person's kidneys and liver are working. These tests may help a doctor figure out what is triggering a person's seizures—for instance, if the person is not getting the right amount of nutrients.

Another test for epilepsy is called a lumbar puncture, also known as a spinal tap. In this test, a doctor takes a sample of the fluid that surrounds the spinal cord and tests it in a lab. The tests "can help in the diagnosis of disorders of the central nervous system that may involve the brain, spinal cord, or their coverings (called the meninges)."[46] These disorders may be causing the person's seizures. If they are, it will affect the person's treatment.

Creating a Treatment Plan

Although medical tests do not always show the cause

of a person's epilepsy, they do provide information that a doctor uses to help the patient decide on the best course of treatment. Treatment for epilepsy aims to rid a person of seizures or cut down on the number of seizures a person has. When people are treated for epilepsy, about six out of ten people will become seizure free within a few years, and about half are seizure free for at least a year after taking their first anti-seizure medication.

Funding Epilepsy Research

Although a number of treatment options exist for people with epilepsy, sometimes a treatment cannot be found. For this reason, researchers are always looking for new types of treatment. In 2002, Warren Lammert and Dr. Orrin Devinsky founded the Epilepsy Therapy Project, which merged with the Epilepsy Foundation in 2012. This project does several things to help doctors discover new therapies, including:

- *Promoting partnerships among industry, academia, investors, and physicians*
- *Providing financial support to advance promising science that could lead to better therapies*
- *Fostering innovation and entrepreneurship so novel epilepsy projects and companies can make it to people with epilepsy*
- *Providing visibility to therapies and devices in the epilepsy pipeline and increase attention to the real needs of people with epilepsy and the need for more research efforts[1]*

1. "Epilepsy Therapy Project," The Epilepsy Foundation, accessed October 18, 2017. www.epilepsy.com/make-difference/research-and-new-therapies/epilepsy-therapy-project.

Because epilepsy is caused by so many different things, many medications and other methods are used to treat it. Epilepsy is an individualized disorder, and no single treatment works in every person who has epilepsy. "Partly because there are so many different causes, we will never have one treatment or one cure that will help everybody with epilepsy," Sucholeiki said. "For the vast majority of people there is no cure; rather, there is treatment."[47] Studies have shown that if the first two or three medications fail to control a person's seizures, it is unlikely that any medication will work for them. At that point, some doctors recommend surgery or other non-drug treatments. The Epilepsy Foundation noted some factors that can improve a person's chances of becoming seizure free with treatment:

- *No known history of brain injury or abnormality*
- *A normal neurological exam and EEG*
- *No family history of epilepsy*
- *Having an unknown cause of epilepsy*[48]

Medical Treatment

"Medicines have come out in the last couple of years that are so well tolerated and safe that it's the first line of treatment,"[49] Sucholeiki said in 2009. Since the 1980s, the medication options for people with epilepsy have dramatically improved. There are more than 20 drug treatments for epilepsy, including Keppra, Zarontin, and Lamictal. According to Singh, "Fifteen or twenty years ago we only had four or five drugs to treat patients. The last ten or fifteen years we've had another ten to twelve medications."[50]

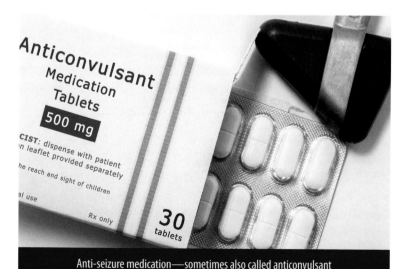

Anti-seizure medication—sometimes also called anticonvulsant medication—helps about 70 percent of epilepsy patients.

Doctors can use a single medication to treat a patient or can combine drugs to give the patient the best chance of being seizure free. It is not always clear which combination is best until the patient tries it, however. Some people respond well to the first medicine they try, while others may need to either add a second medication or try different ones before they find one that works. According to the Epilepsy Foundation, combining more than two drugs generally does not have any effect on a person's epilepsy. "I can look at a person, do all the testing, even see their seizure, and I can't tell which drug they'll respond to," said Carl Bazil, the director of the Epilepsy and Sleep Division of the Department of Neurology and the Columbia Comprehensive Epilepsy Center at the Columbia University Medical Center. "There must be something about their action in the brain, but we don't know what it is."[51]

Epilepsy drugs may carry serious side effects that vary from person to person and medication to medication. One patient may become extremely tired after taking epilepsy medication. Another medication may cause a person to become hyperactive and unable to settle down. Other side effects can include gaining or losing weight as well as becoming dizzy or anemic—a condition in which a person has fewer red blood cells than normal. Osteoporosis or mental disturbances are other potential side effects. When prescribing epilepsy medication, doctors must balance the benefits of the drug treatment with the problems it may cause. Devinsky explained,

You might have two staring spells a month lasting a couple of minutes, and you're on a high dose of medication ... Now, I can put you on a second medication and get you down to one a month. So now you've got two extra minutes a month but in exchange it's affecting your quality of life for the

15 hours a day you're awake: it may make you tired, or dizzy, or cause mood changes or memory problems. So do you want to make that trade-off?[52]

Avoiding Scams

There are some people in the world who take advantage of people's epilepsy. Since there is no cure and some people do not respond well to treatment, they may become desperate and eager to try anything. People should beware of anything promising a cure for epilepsy or guaranteed positive results, such as herbs, medicines, magic, or unusual therapies. Anything that is badly misspelled, not found on a legitimate website—for instance, a comment on a social media post or a banner ad—or promises fast, effective results should be avoided.

In one instance of fraud, Jon C. Sabin sold dogs he claimed could detect seizures before they started. In 2013, the New York supreme court ordered Sabin to stop selling dogs to people, stating that he was clearly not being honest because he would not tell people how he trained the dogs. A legitimate seizure dog trainer will give people that information. At least 12 people came forward after the lawsuit to say that not only did the dogs not detect seizures, they were not obedience trained, although Sabin denied the claims.

When Medicine Fails

A person who does not respond to medication must consider other ways to stop the seizures. Typically, the next treatment option is surgery. During surgery, the part of the brain causing the seizures is removed, leaving the healthy tissue.

Much work is done before surgery to make sure that the portion being removed does not control vital functions. Before surgery, a person goes through an extensive evaluation as the surgeon tries to pinpoint the exact part of the brain that is causing the seizures. Testing is necessary because the precise location is not always apparent by sight or touch during surgery. "If there is a brain tumor or a major developmental malformation, you can see or feel there's something wrong, but in the majority of the cases there's nothing really to be seen,"[53] Singh said.

In addition to EEG monitoring and an MRI scan, a person also undergoes neuropsychological testing before surgery to measure memory, language, and other skills. These tests help doctors determine which part of the brain is not functioning properly. The surgeon can also use a positron-emission tomography (PET) scan to see how well the brain uses glucose, as an area that is not using glucose well could be the site of a person's seizures. A MEG scan can also be used to measure brain activity and provide doctors with a three-dimensional map of the brain. A single photon emission computed tomography (SPECT) scan, which looks at blood flow in the brain, is another evaluation tool doctors may use. "The blood is sent to the most active regions of the brain," Singh explained. "The most blood will be going toward that region with a seizure."[54]

If these tests show that a patient is likely to be helped by surgery, more information is gathered. The Wada test may be used to see whether memory is impaired on one side of the brain. Its official name is the intracarotid sodium amobarbital procedure (ISAP), but most people call it the Wada test after Juhn Wada, the doctor who first performed it. The test involves having a catheter inserted into an artery in the groin, which carries a drug to the brain that puts half of the brain to sleep so the other side of the brain can be tested for memory and language. The test is then repeated for the other side of the brain. The test will show whether memory on one side of the brain has been affected, and it also shows whether the brain can be operated on without harming the person's memory.

A technique called brain mapping can also be used to determine whether the area targeted for surgery controls vital functions such as speech, sight, or movement. While much general information is known about where these functions are located in the brain, many individual variations occur, so it is important to determine where these functions lie in a person's brain before surgery is done. "The exact location of various functions differs quite a bit from person to person," noted the Epilepsy Foundation. "The presence of tumors, seizures, or other brain abnormalities may distort the usual location of some functions. General rules may not ... apply."[55]

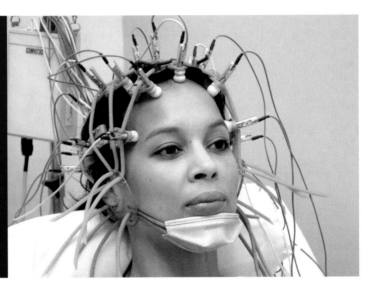

During an EEG, electrodes are placed on the outside of the skull, as shown here. However, sometimes a more accurate test is needed. In that case, electrodes can be temporarily implanted under the skull.

Electrical stimulation of various parts of the brain can be used to see where the vital functions are located. If the area where the seizures are starting is difficult to detect with a test using electrodes on the outside of the skull or if the area is close to a critical functioning area, a doctor can perform surgery to place a grid of electrodes directly onto the surface of the brain to gather information. Depth electrodes that go more deeply into the brain can also be used to help map functions. A small amount of electrical current is sent to the electrodes to determine which functions are controlled by these areas. For example, if a person has trouble speaking when the current is sent to a specific area, it indicates that the area likely controls speech.

During surgery, a doctor removes the part of the brain that is causing the seizures or removes the areas of the brain containing nerve pathways that seizures follow as they spread. Surgery is not a guarantee that a person's seizures will stop, although some patients are free of seizures after surgery. Improvement is typically seen, however.

An Implantable Device

A patient who does not respond to medication and is not a good candidate for surgery has other options for seizure control. One of these is vagus nerve stimulation (VNS). The VNS device has been called a pacemaker for the brain; it is implanted in the chest and sends a mild, brief electrical pulse to the vagus nerve in the neck at certain intervals. For some people, it is every few seconds, while for others, it is every few minutes. The nerve carries the electrical pulse to the brain. It turns off and on automatically; the person using it generally does not notice that it is there, the same way people do not generally pay attention to the fact that they are breathing.

Exactly how the VNS reduces seizures is a mystery. Although it is not considered a cure, the device provides relief for some patients. The Epilepsy Society explained,

VNS therapy aims to reduce the number, length and severity of seizures. For some people their seizures become much less frequent, for some it may reduce their seizures a little, and for others it has no effect. VNS therapy may reduce the length or intensity of seizures but this does not happen for everyone. It may also reduce the time it takes to recover after a seizure. It is unlikely to completely stop seizures and it does not "cure" epilepsy.

The effect of VNS therapy may not happen straight-away; it can take up to two years for it to have an effect on someone's seizures. It is used alongside anti-epileptic drugs (AEDs) not instead of them. However, if VNS therapy works, it may be possible to reduce a person's AEDs over time.[56]

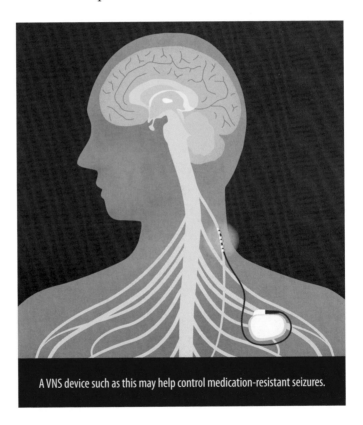

A VNS device such as this may help control medication-resistant seizures.

For James Sandstedt of Texas, the VNS was a life-changing device. Before he had the device implanted at the age of 17, he was averaging more than 100 seizures a night and was extremely exhausted. The high school junior was able to reduce the amount of medication he took after getting the device and became able to enjoy activities he never had the energy for when he was heavily medicated and suffering from numerous seizures. "Before I wasn't really alive, I was just existing," he said. "Now I actually have a life."[57]

Alternatives to Medication

Another method used to control epilepsy is diet. Some children whose epilepsy is resistant to medication are able to control their seizures with the ketogenic diet, which is high in fat but low in carbohydrates. The Epilepsy Society explained how it works:

> Usually the body uses glucose (a form of sugar) from carbohydrates (found in foods like sugar, bread or pasta) for its energy source. Chemicals called ketones are made when the body uses fat for energy (this is called "ketosis") ... Research in 2015 has shown that another chemical, decanoic acid, is also produced as a result of the diet. These chemicals help to reduce seizures for some people.[58]

It is unclear exactly how these chemicals help, but research has shown that it helps about 40 percent of children. For some, it reduced the number of seizures, while for others, it simply made them less lethargic. With this diet, a person eats four times as much fat as carbohydrates and protein combined. It has a low sugar content, which may prevent seizures from forming in the brain. This diet can be complicated, however, and difficult to follow. "You're pretty much eating protein and fat," Singh said. "It is useful, but it can have other consequences, so this is the final option. It's a very cumbersome thing to do, and certainly requires a lot of dedication and discipline."[59] For this reason, the diet is considered a last resort after multiple medications have failed. Another type of diet that is similar but allows people to eat more carbohydrates is called the low glycemic index treatment (LGIT).

With this diet, people can eat carbohydrates that have a low glycemic index, which is a measurement of how high a food raises a person's blood sugar. Foods with a low glycemic index include whole wheat bread, sweet potatoes, and most fruits; foods with a high glycemic index include white bread, popcorn, and potatoes.

The ketogenic diet is low in carbohydrates and high in fat and protein. It can be difficult to follow, but it may help some children with epilepsy whose seizures are resistant to medication.

Another option that is currently being studied is the use of medical marijuana to control seizures. Because marijuana has only recently become legal in parts of the United States, not much research has been done on the effectiveness of medical marijuana. However, preliminary studies show that it may be useful in controlling seizures. The two active ingredients in marijuana are tetrahydrocannabinol (THC) and cannabidiol (CBD). THC is the ingredient that creates changes in awareness associated with "getting high," while CBD has been shown to have positive effects on certain physical and mental conditions, such as chronic pain, epilepsy, and anxiety. For this reason, strains of marijuana are being bred without THC so people can get the medical benefits without getting high. Additionally, concentrated forms of CBD are being developed, such as cannabis oil. For epilepsy, a drug called Epidiolex is being developed from CBD oil. A study of Epidiolex that was published in *Lancet Neurology* showed that it reduced seizures by about 54 percent in people whose epilepsy did not respond to the treatments that are currently available. Other studies have shown similar positive results.

However, medical experts warn that people should not smoke marijuana in an effort to reduce their seizures without their doctor's consultation and supervision. Doing so carries a number of risks, including:

- The marijuana plant contains both THC and CBD, so the high may impair a person's daily functions.
- The amount of these ingredients varies from plant to plant; in contrast, Epidiolex has a regulated amount of CBD, so people are always aware of how much they are taking.
- Marijuana may interact in dangerous and unexpected ways with the anti-seizure medications a person is currently taking.
- Smoke inhalation can put a person at risk for asthma, bronchitis, and other ailments.
- In young adults whose brains have not finished developing, marijuana can have serious negative effects, such as impaired memory.
- Marijuana is still illegal in most of the United States, and being caught with it can result in high fines or jail time. In places where it is legal for medical use, a prescription is required. As of September 2017, only eight states allow people to purchase it for recreational use, and they all require people to be 21 or older to do so.

In states where marijuana is legal for medical use, a person with epilepsy who is of legal age, has discussed the risks and benefits with their doctor, and has obtained a prescription may use marijuana to control their seizures.

Control Is the Goal

Diet, medication, surgery, or an implanted device may help a person become free of seizures or reduce the number or intensity of their seizures. A person who has seizures as a child may outgrow them; about half of children who have epilepsy are taken off medication after several years. "It's likely that one way people outgrow it is that the childhood brain is prone to excess electrical activity," Sucholeiki said. "As the brain matures, it has its own mechanisms to dampen the excessive activity."[60]

For those whose epilepsy is permanent, seizure control is the goal. "Most people with epilepsy will live normal lives once their seizures are controlled,"[61] Singh noted. However, some people with epilepsy do not respond to any current treatments. These patients are still waiting for a treatment that will control their seizures and allow them to live life without worrying about their next seizure.

CHAPTER FIVE

ONGOING RESEARCH

The fact that epilepsy has no cure frustrates many people, even those who have control over their seizures. Additionally, people with epilepsy have varying ideas of what can be considered control. A poll conducted in 2016 by the Epilepsy Foundation showed that some people with epilepsy consider their seizures to be controlled if they only happen at night, do not impact their daily activities, or are reduced by quite a lot. However, the Epilepsy Foundation considers seizure control to mean having zero seizures after starting treatment.

"Treatments are band aids designed to treat the expression of the disorder," noted William Davis Gaillard, "but they do not treat the underlying disorder."[62] Treatments may also have negative side effects that are better than seizures but still not pleasant. For this reason, researchers are working on understanding more about the causes of epilepsy so they can target treatments more effectively and perhaps one day discover a cure.

Studying Genes

One way researchers hope to learn more about epilepsy is by studying the genetic makeup of people with epilepsy. Genes carry instructions for determining how the body is built, and some genes are associated with disorders. The Epilepsy Phenome/Genome

Project (EPGP) and a related project called Epi4K, sponsored by the National Institutes of Health (NIH) and the National Institute of Neurological Disorders and Stroke (NINDS), have worked to identify genes that contribute to a person developing epilepsy. They are also looking at how certain genes respond to seizure medications. EPGP was launched in 2007, and Epi4k was launched in 2012.

To gather the genetic information, researchers collect blood samples from people who have certain types of epilepsy as well as siblings who have epilepsy. They also gather information about people's seizure histories. Researchers hope the information provided through this study will contribute to an understanding of the chemical processes in the body that lead to epilepsy as well as improvements in diagnosis and treatment. The information the study provides will help doctors decide which drugs will be most effective and have the fewest side effects for a patient.

Researchers hope genetic testing will one day reveal a cure for epilepsy.

Genetic technology has the potential to unlock the cause of epilepsy in a number of cases. Although knowing the genetic makeup of epilepsy will make treatments more effective, Gaillard estimates it could take decades before that happens. One day, however, it may be possible to treat the genes that cause problems in a significant number of people with epilepsy rather than using medication to treat the seizure. "The genetics revolution is going to change how we view epilepsy," he predicted. "Eventually we will be able to identify patients at risk for side effects from certain medications and it will also allow us to be more precise in knowing which medications will work for a certain child rather than the random way we treat children now."[63] As of 2013, 4,223 participants were enrolled in the studies, and 25 genetic mutations had been identified on 9 genes.

New Types of Treatment

While research is being done to help doctors match an epilepsy patient with the right medication, research is also being done to improve the medications available. Epilepsy medications often come with unwanted side effects, and researchers are looking into new drug treatments that reduce seizures without producing significant side effects.

At the University of Wisconsin–Madison, researchers are trying to create a drug that will mimic the ketogenic diet that some people have found to be effective in reducing seizures. They are using a compound with a chemical structure similar to sugar that blocks sugar metabolism in the brain and prevents the body from using glucose. The cells think they are taking in glucose, but the compound stops them from actually doing so. Dr. Thomas Sutula, one of the researchers, said the compound, which is called 2-deoxy-glucose (2DG), is "remarkably safe." He said, "It's about as close to a natural product as you can get without being a natural product."[64]

The way a drug is delivered may also change in the future. Epilepsy medications are typically in pill form, which causes the medication to travel through the organs and the rest of the body to get to the brain. A new method of delivering medication would deliver the medicine directly to the brain. To get the medication there, a treatment pump or another device would send the drug or an electrical signal to the area in the brain where a person's seizures develop. Studies are ongoing with both of these treatments to make sure they are safe and effective for humans.

Tests are also being done with the responsive neurostimulator system (RNS), which is a battery-controlled device that is implanted under the scalp and programmed to detect a seizure before it begins. The brain changes in subtle ways prior to a seizure. It is hoped that the device will sense these changes so medication or an electrical signal can be sent before the seizure begins and stop it before it starts. The U.S. Food and Drug Administration (FDA) has approved it for use in medical facilities, but it is hoped that eventually it will be made more widely available.

Another treatment being studied is deep brain stimulation (DBS), which has been used to treat illnesses such as Parkinson's disease, anxiety, depression, and obsessive-compulsive disorder (OCD). It is generally used when these disorders are resistant to other forms of treatment. DBS uses an electrode implanted in the brain to deliver a pulse to the brain. There are some questions about which areas to stimulate, however, and the treatment has varied results in people with epilepsy. According to the Epilepsy Foundation, further research will be aimed at answering the following questions:

- *What brain targets for DBS are the most effective for controlling seizures, and how effective is DBS for epilepsy?*
- *Can DBS reliably suppress the start of seizures, rapidly terminate seizures, or both?*

- *Are all epilepsy syndromes and seizure types equally responsive to DBS?*
- *What stimulation parameters are best for controlling seizures?*
- *Is there a way to detect when seizures start in the brain and deliver the stimulation only when needed?*
- *Can medication doses be reduced in patients receiving DBS therapy?*[65]

Advancements are also being made in surgical instruments used in brain surgery. One advancement for epilepsy patients undergoing surgery is Gamma Knife Radiosurgery. The Gamma Knife can be used to treat seizures that are focused in certain areas of the brain. "Instead of cutting pieces of the brain out, you can burn them through radiation,"[66] Singh explained.

Although it is called a knife, the instrument actually uses targeted beams of radiation to remove a tumor or area of the brain. No incision is made; rather, doctors focus beams of radiation on the area of the brain that needs to be removed, thus protecting the surrounding tissue from harm. The procedure allows a patient to avoid having part of the skull removed, as it would be in traditional brain surgery, which decreases the patient's pain and stress as well as improves recovery time after surgery. However, it can include side effects, including a temporary increase in seizures.

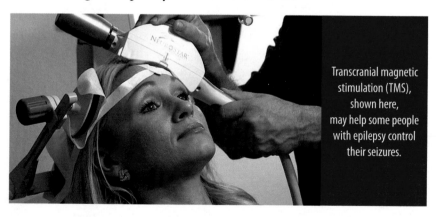

Transcranial magnetic stimulation (TMS), shown here, may help some people with epilepsy control their seizures.

An Experimental Product

The Monarch eTNS System is a product that provides a low level of electrical stimulation to the trigeminal nerve. The trigeminal nerve controls muscles around the jaw that are used for chewing and is also responsible for the transmission of sensations to the nasal cavity, teeth, mouth, and face. Unlike a VNS device, it is not implantable; it is a small patch that can be attached to the patient's forehead, which means it can be used at home. It is intended to be used in addition to medication or other treatment. The creators of the eTNS system have reported that 40 percent of people who use the device experienced half their usual number of seizures after 18 weeks of treatment. The eTNS device has been approved for sale in Europe, Canada, and Australia, but it has not yet been approved in the United States; tests are still ongoing to verify the company's claims.

New Ways to Look at the Brain

Surgeons are aided by machines that allow them to look inside the brain, and advancements are also being made in the tools that give doctors a more detailed picture of the structure of a person's brain. Improvements in MRI machines are giving doctors a clearer image of what things look like beneath the skull. As the MRI machines become more powerful, they produce images that show more subtle abnormalities in a person's brain. Using an increased number of different MRI sequences provides doctors such as Gaillard with more data to use. "More information can be gleaned from those kinds of technologies, and that is only going to increase over the next few years,"[67] he said.

The strength of the magnet in the imaging device is measured in teslas, with many community hospitals having an MRI of 1.5 tesla. An epilepsy center generally has a stronger imaging device of 3 tesla or even 6 tesla. "The stronger the magnet, the better the pictures,"[68] Singh explained. There are a few MRI machines that use magnets between 7 and 11 tesla, but as of 2017, these were very rare. The clearer the picture of a person's brain, the more information doctors will be able to learn about where seizures originate and help identify areas to avoid during an operation.

Using Technology

Technological advances have helped people with epilepsy in their everyday life. One such advancement is called the Hövding, which was created in 2005 by two Swedish women as an alternative to bicycle helmets. Some people do not like the way helmets feel, while others are concerned with looking unstylish. In order to address this issue, Hövding is a collar the cyclist can wear around the neck. It automatically inflates like an airbag to protect the head and neck when it senses the wearer's body position change in response to a fall. It has been suggested as an alternative to epilepsy helmets as well. Hövding has been proven effective and comes in a variety of colors and patterns, but it may be too expensive for many people to afford. Additionally, its current design allows it to be used only once; the airbag cannot be put back into the collar after it inflates. This would make it unhelpful for people who have multiple drop seizures. The inventors are working on making a reusable helmet, but if they succeed, it will be several years before it is available for purchase.

Another way technology can help people with epilepsy is through apps. Some of these include:

- HealthUnlocked, which connects people who have similar health conditions. This allows them to share advice and give support to each other.
- Seizure First Aide, which gives step-by-step first aid instructions to anyone who witnesses a seizure.
- Snug Safety, which checks in with the person every day. If they do not respond to the app, it sends an alert to the person's emergency contacts.

This is especially helpful for people with epilepsy who live alone.

- ICE Medical Standard, which allows someone to put their emergency medical information on their phone's lock screen so first responders can access it even when the phone is locked.
- Epilepsy Journal, which allows people to track information about their seizures—start and end time, number of seizures per day, possible triggers, and other important details—in order to control them better.
- Neurology Now, which, in addition to tracking seizures, includes tools such as a medication reminder and other features to help people with epilepsy achieve better seizure control.
- SeizAlarm, which alerts the person's emergency contacts if the person needs help. The person can do this by sending an alert if they think they will need help soon, or the app can send an automatic alert if it detects seizure-like motions or increased heart rate. The person's location is sent in a help request so they can be found easily.

More to Do

Although many exciting advancements are being made in the tools used to diagnose and treat epilepsy, one of the challenges to finding a cure for epilepsy is money. In fiscal year 2017 (October 2016 to September 2017), the Centers for Disease Control and Prevention (CDC) set aside $8.5 million for epilepsy research. There are about 3 million adults living with epilepsy, so this works out to about $2 for each person. Although extra money comes from people donating to organizations such as the Epilepsy Foundation, some question the level of funding for epilepsy research. "The investment in research by the federal government and the investment of private dollars in epilepsy research have simply not been proportional to the burden of this disease,"[69] wrote Susan Axelrod, whose daughter, Lauren, began suffering epileptic seizures at seven months old.

Eager to see advancements made in epilepsy treatment, Axelrod and others whose lives have been impacted by the disease founded Citizens United for Research in Epilepsy (CURE). The organization raises money and supports researchers looking for a cure for epilepsy. "We want complete freedom from seizures," Axelrod said. "We want future families to be spared what so many other families, for so many years, have endured. Lives should not be defined by diseases."[70]

CURE has a goal of eliminating the side effects people experience as a result of taking anti-seizure medication as well as getting rid of seizures. It is especially interested in preventing epilepsy, stopping it from occurring in people with brain injuries, and reversing the cognitive impact frequent seizures can have on the brain. Other research supported by CURE looks at ways of minimizing the risk of SUDEP.

With funding from CURE, researchers have investigated new treatments for seizures caused by brain injury, ways to prevent seizures after a brain injury, and how heart problems may be linked to SUDEP. Research has also been conducted on new diet therapies for epilepsy, a link between breathing control and SUDEP, and using viral technology to impact the neurotransmitters in the brain and give people freedom from seizures. Other researchers are looking at ways to better treat newborn babies who have seizures. All over the world, researchers assisted by CURE are working to find a solution to the puzzles of epilepsy and to allow people to live without seizures or side effects from anti-seizure medications.

The Need for Trigger Warnings

Not everyone with epilepsy has the same triggers, but flashing lights are a common, known trigger. In some cases, they are easy to avoid, but in others, they may be unexpected. For instance, some episodes of the Netflix show *Stranger Things* could potentially cause seizures, and some GIFs flash so quickly that they can also be triggering. For these reasons, people with photosensitive epilepsy generally appreciate being warned in advance that something may trigger their seizures so they can avoid looking at it. Many people are advocating for shows and movies to use trigger warnings when necessary, and some feel the creators should avoid flashing lights entirely, as they sometimes make people with epilepsy miss out on media they would otherwise enjoy watching.

Some people without epilepsy do not think to put trigger warnings on things, while others may resent being asked to do it. They may believe it is the responsibility of a person with epilepsy to avoid things that will cause seizures. To some extent, this is true; if someone knows something will trigger a seizure, they should avoid it, and people with epilepsy generally do because they do not enjoy their seizures. However, they cannot avoid something they know nothing about, which is why trigger warnings are helpful. They are also very easy for content creators to make, although tagging something with #epilepsy on social media is generally unhelpful because sometimes people with epilepsy search the tag to find text posts about it. It is more helpful to use tags such as #seizurewarning, #gifwarning, or #flashinggif. A person can also use #epilepsywarning as long as the tag is all one word; tagging it as two separate words will cause it to show up in the regular #epilepsy tag.

Some scenes in *Stranger Things* could potentially cause seizures. Many people who have photosensitive epilepsy want media with flashing lights to be clearly labeled so they can avoid it.

Raising Awareness

People with epilepsy have input into finding a cure as well when they become actively involved in managing their health care, giving feedback about their treatments to their doctor, and participating in research studies. "It becomes more and more evident that it won't be just the doctors, researchers, and scientists pushing the field forward," said Frances E. Jensen, chair of the department of neurology at Penn Medicine. "There's an active role for parents and patients. They tell us when the drugs aren't working."[71]

As people with epilepsy and their family members discuss the disorder with others and raise awareness of the severity of the problem, they, too, are involved in the search for a cure. Although epilepsy impacts the lives of millions of people, the disorder often remains hidden and misunderstood. "Because most people with epilepsy are not in a constant state of seizure—they are, rather, in perpetual but quiet danger—their condition can appear less serious than it truly is,"[72] noted former *Newsweek* editor Jon Meacham in an article on epilepsy and its impact.

While some people think epilepsy is not serious, others believe epilepsy is such a burden that it prevents people from performing normal activities. This misperception is harmful because it further impacts the quality of life of someone with epilepsy. For instance, the CDC reported that in 2013, 12 percent of adults in the United States said they would avoid someone with uncontrolled epilepsy. Additionally, during the 2016 presidential campaign, "a video clip of [Democratic nominee Hillary] Clinton was circulated along with claims that it showed her experiencing a brief seizure and proved she was ill and unfit to hold office."[73] This claim proved two things. First, it showed that many people are uninformed about what a seizure truly looks like because Clinton's motor actions were clearly under her control in the video. Second, it showed the stigma that persists around epilepsy, as the incident was used in an attempt to discredit Clinton's presidential campaign. Although Clinton does not have epilepsy, she would not be unfit to be president if she did.

To get rid of the misperceptions about epilepsy, more people will need to be educated about this brain disorder. From videos of everyday people on YouTube to comments from Hollywood celebrities, more people are encouraging others to engage in the discussion about epilepsy. To bring more information to high school students, the Epilepsy Foundation offers a program called Seizures and You: Take Charge of the Facts. Another version called Seizures and You: Take Charge of the Storm is aimed at middle school students. The 45-minute programs, which consist of a short video and class discussion, have been shown to make a significant difference in the way people look at the condition. "We have excellent data that young people who go through this program come away with a completely different understanding,"[74] Hargis said in reference to Take Charge of the Facts. Teachers can contact the Epilepsy Foundation to order a program kit.

Helping more people understand what epilepsy is and the impact it makes on people's lives will help raise awareness of the condition and what it means for people who live with the seizure disorder. Greater acceptance can ease the social implications of epilepsy and foster greater understanding of what it means to live with the condition every day.

Making more people aware of what it is like to have epilepsy also raises awareness of the importance of getting seizures under control. This gives people with epilepsy the freedom to pursue their dreams and ambitions. "It's certainly a serious medical condition, no doubt about it, but most people live normal lives once their seizures are controlled,"[75] Singh said.

Introduction:
A Misunderstood Disorder

1. Steven C. Schachter, Patricia O. Shafer, and Joseph I. Sirven, "What Is a Seizure?," Epilepsy Foundation, last updated March 19, 2014. www.epilepsy.com/learn/about-epilepsy-basics/what-seizure.

2. Sanjay Singh, telephone interview by Terri Dougherty, May 13, 2009.

3. Eric Hargis, telephone interview by Terri Dougherty, May 26, 2009.

Chapter One:
What Is Epilepsy?

4. Orrin Devinsky, *A Guide to Understanding and Living with Epilepsy*. Philadelphia, PA: F.A. Davis Company, 1994, p.3.

5. Roy Sucholeiki, telephone interview by Terri Dougherty, May 11, 2009.

6. Sucholeiki, interview.

7. Sucholeiki, interview.

8. Jerry Adler, "Epilepsy: Life on the Frontlines," *Newsweek*, April 10, 2009. www.newsweek.com/epilepsy-life-frontlines-77383.

9. "Epilepsy FAQ's," Epilepsy Care and Research Foundation, accessed October 27, 2017. www.epilepsycareandresearchfoundation.com/epilepsy-and-pregnancy-faq.html.

10. Quoted in Ali Venosa, "Epilepsy May Be Causing More Deaths Than We Realize,

Thanks to Underreporting," *Medical Daily*, December 16, 2015. www.medicaldaily.com/epilepsy-may-be-causing-more-deaths-we-realize-thanks-underreporting-365618.

11. "SUDEP," Epilepsy Foundation, last updated July 21, 2014. www.epilepsy.com/learn/early-death-and-sudep/sudep.

12. Sucholeiki, interview.

13. Sucholeiki, interview.

14. Hargis, interview.

15. Tony Coelho, "Epilepsy Gave Me a Mission," *Exceptional Parent*, March 1995.

16. Hargis, interview.

17. Hargis, interview.

Chapter Two:
Different Types of Seizures

18. Anahad O'Connor, "The Claim: During a Seizure, You Can Swallow Your Tongue," *New York Times*, April 22, 2008. www.nytimes.com/2008/04/22/health/22real.html.

19. Sucholeiki, interview.

20. Steven C. Schachter, Patricia O. Shafer, and Joseph I. Sirven, "What Are the Risk Factors?," Epilepsy Foundation, last updated March 19, 2014. www.epilepsy.com/101/ep101_risks.

21. Sucholeiki, interview.

22. Elaine Kiriakopoulous and Patricia O. Shafer, "Types of Seizures," Epilepsy Foundation, last updated March 20, 2017. www.epilepsy.com/learn/types-seizures.

23. Orrin Devinsky and Joseph I. Sirven, "Myoclonic Seizures," Epilepsy Foundation, last

updated March 19, 2013. www.epilepsy.com/learn/types-seizures/myoclonic-seizures.

24. Donald Weaver, *Epilepsy and Seizures: Everything You Need to Know.* Buffalo, NY: Firefly, 2001, p. 33.

25. Singh, interview.

26. Elaine Kiriakopoulos and Patricia O. Shafer, "Focal Onset Impaired Awareness Seizures (Complex Partial Seizures)," Epilepsy Foundation, last updated March 23, 2017. w w w . e p i l e p s y . c o m / l e a r n / t y p e s - seizures/focal-onset-impaired-awareness- seizures-aka-complex-partial-seizures.

27. Steven C. Schachter, Patricia O. Shafer, and Joseph I. Sirven, "What Happens During a Seizure?," Epilepsy Foundation, last updated March 19, 2014. www.epilepsy.com/learn/ about-epilepsy-basics/what-happens-during- seizure.

28. Sucholeiki, interview.

Chapter Three:
The Truth About Epilepsy

29. B.J. Hamrick, telephone interview by Terri Dougherty, May 11, 2009.

30. Hamrick, interview.

31. Hamrick, interview.

32. Hamrick, interview.

33. Hamrick, interview.

34. Hamrick, interview.

35. Hamrick, interview.

36. Heather Good, telephone interview by Terri Dougherty, May 12, 2009.

37. Good, interview.

38. Good, interview.

39. Good, interview.

40. Good, interview.

41. Good, interview.

42. Good, interview.

Chapter Four: Analysis and Treatment

43. Singh, interview.

44. Ruben Kuzniecky and Joseph I. Sirven, "MEG (Magnetoencephalography)," Epilepsy Foundation, August 13, 2013. www.epilepsy.com/learn/diagnosis/looking-brain/meg-magneto-encephalography.

45. Singh, interview.

46. Neil Lava, "Epilepsy and the Spinal Tap," WebMD, June 10, 2017. www.webmd.com/epilepsy/guide/epilepsy-spinal-tap#2.

47. Sucholeiki, interview.

48. Steven C. Schachter, Patricia O. Shafer, and Joseph I. Sirven, "Will I Always Have Seizures?," Epilepsy Foundation, last updated March 19, 2014. www.epilepsy.com/learn/about-epilepsy-basics/will-i-always-have-seizures.

49. Sucholeiki, interview.

50. Singh, interview.

51. Quoted in Adler, "Epilepsy: Life on the Frontlines."

52. Quoted in Adler, "Epilepsy: Life on the Frontlines."

53. Singh, interview.

54. Singh, interview.

55. Howard L. Weiner and Joseph I. Sirven, "Brain Mapping," Epilepsy Foundation, last updated August 25, 2013. www.epilepsy.com/learn/ treating-seizures-and-epilepsy/surgery/pre-surgery-tests/brain-mapping.

56. "Vagus Nerve Stimulation," Epilepsy Society, November 2016. www.epilepsysociety.org.uk/ vagus-nerve-stimulation#.WekJOmXse-I.

57. James Sandstedt, telephone interview by Terri Dougherty, May 24, 2009.

58. "Ketogenic Diet," Epilepsy Society, March 2016. www.epilepsysociety.org.uk/ ketogenic-diet#.Wen9_2Xse-J.

59. Singh, interview.

60. Sucholeiki, interview.

61. Singh, interview.

Chapter Five: Ongoing Research

62. William Davis Gaillard, telephone interview by Terri Dougherty, June 12, 2009.

63. Gaillard, interview.

64. Quoted in David Wahlberg, "New (Old) Twist in Fight Against Epilepsy Research at UW–Madison Is Exploring a Treatment from Biblical Times," Madison.com, February 14, 2009. host.madison.com/news/new-old-twist-in-fight-against-epilepsy-research-at-uw/ article_5880346e-457c-5741-9981-de643e9d-18eb.html.

65. "The Cutting Edge: Research in Deep Brain Stimulation for Epilepsy," Epilepsy Foundation, accessed October 19, 2017.

www.epilepsy.com/article/2014/3/cutting-edge-research-deep-brain-stimulation-epilepsy.

66. Singh, interview.

67. Gaillard, interview.

68. Singh, interview.

69. Susan Axelrod, "Agony, Hope, and Resolve," *Newsweek*, April 20, 2009, p. 49.

70. Quoted in Jon Meacham, "A Storm in the Brain," *Newsweek*, April 20, 2009, p. 41.

71. Quoted in Melissa Fay Greene, "I Must Save My Child," *Parade*, February 15, 2009. www.parade.com/health/2009/02/susan-axelrod-CURE-epilepsy.html.

72. Meacham, "A Storm in the Brain," p. 40.

73. Dan Evon, "I'm with Seiz-Her," Snopes, July 23, 2016. www.snopes.com/hillary-clinton-seizure-video/.

74. Hargis, interview.

75. Singh, interview.

absence seizure: A seizure involving a brief loss of awareness, generally characterized by staring.

atonic seizure: A seizure involving weakness and loss of muscle strength.

aura: The warning symptoms of a seizure. Not all seizures start with an aura.

clonic seizure: A seizure that impacts muscles on both sides of the body and involves jerking movements.

electroencephalograph (EEG): A test used in diagnosing epilepsy that uses a machine to record the brain's electrical activity.

focal onset seizure: A seizure involving only one part of the brain.

focal to bilateral tonic-clonic seizure: A seizure that starts in one part of the brain and spreads to both sides.

generalized seizure: A seizure involving both sides of the brain.

ketogenic diet: A diet high in fat and low in carbohydrates. It has been successful in controlling seizures in some children.

magnetic resonance imaging (MRI): A scanning technique that uses a strong magnet to produce pictures of the brain.

magnetoencephalograph (MEG): A technique that uses the brain's magnetic activity to produce an image of the brain.

myoclonic seizure: A seizure that involves one or more brief jerks that last for about a second

single photon emission computed tomography (SPECT): A test that looks at blood flow in the brain.

tonic seizure: A type of seizure that involves stiffening of the muscles on both sides of the body. A person generally remains conscious during the seizure.

tonic-clonic seizure: A seizure involving stiffening of muscles, falling, and jerking. A person loses consciousness during the seizure.

American Epilepsy Society
135 South LaSalle St., Suite 2850
Chicago, IL 60603
(312) 883-3800
www.aesnet.org
This organization for neurological professionals
promotes the exchange of information about epilepsy.
It offers information about epilepsy research and grants
and, through its website, helps patients find a doctor.
It also has an online database of information from its
annual meetings.

Citizens United for Research in Epilepsy (CURE)
430 West Erie, Suite 210
Chicago, IL 60654
(312) 255-1801
www.cureepilepsy.org
This volunteer-based, nonprofit organization was
founded by parents of children with epilepsy who
are focused on finding a cure. It produces newsletters
several times a year, and its website provides links to
other epilepsy resources and articles about epilepsy.

Epilepsy Foundation
8301 Professional Place East, Suite 200
Landover, MD 20785
(800) 332-1000
www.epilepsy.com
This national voluntary agency promotes research for
a cure for epilepsy. It offers programs throughout the
United States as it works to improve the way people
with epilepsy are perceived and ensures that people with
seizures can participate in life experiences. It produces
pamphlets about epilepsy for health care professionals
and people with epilepsy. Its website also contains a list
of books and other media about epilepsy.

International League Against Epilepsy
342 North Main Street
West Hartford, CT 06117
(860) 586-7547
www.ilae-epilepsy.org
Founded in 1909, this organization spreads information
about epilepsy and promotes research, education, and
training. It also aims to improve services to those with
epilepsy and care for patients through prevention,
diagnosis, and treatment.

National Association of Epilepsy Centers (NAEC)
600 Maryland Avenue SW, Suite 835 W
Washington, D.C. 20024
(202) 524-6767
info@naec-epilepsy.org
www.naec-epilepsy.org
This organization is the voice of epilepsy centers
across the United States. It also works to get the
federal government to provide more financial support
for epilepsy programs and more services for people who
have epilepsy.

FOR MORE INFORMATION

Books

Bazil, Carl W. *Living Well with Epilepsy and Other Seizure Disorders: An Expert Explains What You Really Need to Know*. New York, NY: HarperCollins, 2004. This book offers treatment options, support, and answers for people living with epilepsy.

Bjorklund, Ruth. *Epilepsy*. Tarrytown, NY: Marshall Cavendish Benchmark, 2007. This book offers easy-to-understand information about epilepsy.

Devinsky, Orrin. *Epilepsy: Patient and Family Guide (3rd Edition)*. New York, NY: Demos Medical, 2007. Written by a leading expert in epilepsy, this guide for patients offers insightful information and answers common questions about the disorder.

Gay, Kathlyn, and Sean McGarrahan. *Epilepsy: The Ultimate Teen Guide (2nd Edition)*. Lanham: Rowman & Littlefield, 2017. This book helps teens take charge of their epilepsy. It includes information about treatment and management as well as ways the Americans with Disabilities Act affects people with the disorder.

Schachter, Steven C., and Lisa Francesca Andermann. *Epilepsy in Our World: Stories of Living with Seizures from Around the World*. Cambridge, UK: Oxford University Press, 2008. This book explores the similarities and differences of life with epilepsy in cultures around the world.

Websites

About Kids Health: Epilepsy
www.aboutkidshealth.ca/En/JustForKids/Health/
Epilepsy/Pages/default.aspx
Through an interactive cartoon, visitors learn what it
is like to have epilepsy and can take a short quiz to test
their knowledge.

Brain Anatomy
www.koshland-science-museum.org/explore-the-
science/interactives/brain-anatomy
This interactive website features both an external and
internal model of the brain.

Centers for Disease Control and Prevention
www.cdc.gov
This website offers information on many health issues.
Search for "epilepsy" to find a definition of the disorder,
basic information, statistics, and resources.

National Institute of Neurological Disorders and Stroke
www.ninds.nih.gov
This institute offers information on a number of
disorders impacting the brain, including epilepsy.

Talk About It!
www.talkaboutit.org
Through videos, this website explains what epilepsy is
and offers support for those who have it.

INDEX

PICTURE CREDITS

Cover (main) Keith Brofsky/Photodisc/Getty Images; cover, back cover, pp. 1, 2–3, 4–5, 6, 9, 11, 20, 24, 25, 32, 38, 45, 48, 51, 55, 58, 60, 63, 72, 77, 81, 84, 90, 92, 94, 96, 103, 104 (purple texture) wongwean/Shutterstock.com; back cover (texture) Evannovostro/Shutterstock.com; p. 7 DEA/G. DAGLI ORTI/De Agostini Picture Library/Getty Images; p. 10 Courtesy of the Library of Congress; p. 12 Maridav/Shutterstock.com; p. 13 David Tadevosian/Shutterstock.com; p. 15 Tefi/Shutterstock.com; p. 18 Juriah Mosin/Shutterstock.com; p. 20 Paras Griffin/WireImage/Getty Images; p. 23 sirtravelalot/Shutterstock.com; p. 26 Joe Amon/The Denver Post via Getty Images; p. 27 Pavel Ilyukhin/Shutterstock.com; p. 30 BlueRingMedia/Shutterstock.com; p. 33 Veronika Zakharova/Shutterstock.com; p. 37 Tina Stallard/The Image Bank/Getty Image; p. 39 MJTH/Shutterstock.com; p. 41 Lopolo/Shutterstock.com; p. 43 melis/Shutterstock.com; p. 47 gpointstudio/Shutterstock.com; p. 49 NoPainNoGain/Shutterstock.com; p. 53 © iStockphoto.com/asiseeit; p. 56 Chaikom/Shutterstock.com; p. 59 Steve Snowden/Shutterstock.com; p. 61 Shidlovski/Shutterstock.com; p. 65 BSIP/UIG/Universal Images Group/Getty Images; p. 67 chombosan/Shutterstock.com; p. 69 Elena Shashkina/Shutterstock.com; p. 73 Chepko Danil Vitalevich/Shutterstock.com; p. 76 Sean Pitts/Orlando Sentinel/MCT via Getty Images; p. 81 ©Netflix/courtesy Everett Collection.

ABOUT THE AUTHOR

Simon Pierce grew up in Jamestown, New York. He later moved to New York City and completed his education at NYU. He now lives in Brooklyn with his partner and their son. He has written for various health and wellness publications over the past seven years. He and his family enjoy people-watching in the park or reading the names on cemetery headstones and inventing stories about them.